Adolf Grünbaum

# The Repression of Psychoanalysis

# THE REPRESSION OF PSYCHOANALYSIS

## Otto Fenichel and the Political Freudians

RUSSELL JACOBY

BASIC BOOKS, INC., PUBLISHERS

NEW YORK

Library of Congress Cataloging in Publication Data

Jacoby, Russell.
    The repression of psychoanalysis.

    Includes bibliographical references and index.
    1.  Psychoanalysis—Social aspects.  2.  Fenichel,
Otto.  3.  Freud, Sigmund, 1856–1939.  I.  Title.
BF175.J28  1983      150.19'52      83–70756
ISBN 0–465–06916–9

For Naomi—again

# CONTENTS

*vii*

# Contents

# PREFACE

THE SPECTER of psychoanalysis continues to haunt society; few, however, are frightened. Over the years the ghost has become a ghost of itself. It traded a threatening, sometimes revolutionary, mien for an affable comportment. At the end of his career, one of the deans of American psychoanalysis, Clarence P. Oberndorf, who had studied with Freud in the early 1920s, reflected with some disappointment that psychoanalysis had turned "legitimate and respectable" as well as "sluggish and smug." Once incorporated into medical schools, psychoanalysis came to attract those who "find security in conformity and propriety."

Oberndorf drew these conclusions three decades ago, in 1953, in his *History of Psychoanalysis in America*. In the interim they have not lost their truth; on the contrary, they have gained truth and lost meaning. History often proceeds not by refuting past insights, but by depriving them of referents; in so doing, those insights are undercut, and lose the ability both to convince and to attract attention. They become inexplicable pronouncements from another era. Today, it is no longer apparent that psychoanalysis was ever rebellious or that it was ever anything but sluggish and smug.

At the moment Oberndorf passed his judgments, Robert Lindner, a Baltimore analyst, confirmed them; he denounced psychoanalysis for succumbing to the conformist spirit sweeping America. Lindner, now almost forgotten, bucked the analytic and cultural trends of the 1950s in a series of books, *Rebel without a Cause, Prescription for Rebellion, Must You Conform?* Hardly a typical analyst, Lindner was an isolated figure, and when he died at the youthful age of forty-one in 1956, he had few analytic allies and no successors.

My account of the repression of psychoanalysis closes with a discussion of Robert Lindner. He stood at the end, perhaps beyond the end, of a long and far-reaching tradition of dissenting and political Freudians. Categorization is inseparable from miscategorization; I realize it is misleading to label these analysts as "political Freudians," as if they constituted some distinct subspecies of psychoanalysis. Rather, the political Freudians were heirs to and representatives of classical psychoanalysis, and they shared its fate; they sank into the psychoanalytic unconscious. When they are remembered, they are only half-remembered.

Today the careful clinical and theoretical works of an Otto Fenichel or an Edith Jacobson or an Annie Reich appear to exemplify the best of main-line psychoanalysis. Yet this perception is incomplete to the point of falsehood; in fact, the misperception is mute proof of the repression and self-repression of psychoanalysis. An entire dimension of the lives of these analysts has fallen into obscurity. They were not only sterling examples of establishment psychoanalysis; they were also political and analytic rebels.

The story of Otto Fenichel and a circle of analysts that included Edith Jacobson and Annie Reich exposes a virtually unknown chapter in the often strange history of psychoanalysis. As fascism drove them out of central Europe, Fenichel secretly rallied and led a number of opposition analysts. For over a decade, until 1945, Fenichel sent out *Rundbriefe* ("round letters") to a band of analysts who shared his political and analytic orientation. The letters were secret; and insofar as Fenichel counseled recipients to destroy them, few outside his circle knew of the letters or the group. Through these communications Fenichel's circle kept alive a political and subversive psychoanalysis—to little avail. By the time of Lindner's lonely protest, Fenichel's group no longer encroached on the consciousness of psychoanalysis.

The theoretical commitments of the political Freudians did not mark them as pariahs or eccentrics; rather, they fairly represented the second generation of psychoanalysts, and more, they fairly represented classical psychoanalysis. Like them, Freud himself valued psychoanalysis more as a general theory of civilization than as an individual treatment; to be sure, it was both. Even if the insights (and myths) contained in Freud's major texts—*The Future of an Illusion* or *Civilization and Its Discontents*—were derived from a therapeutic situation, they went far beyond it. To this spirit of audacious theorizing the political Freudians remained devoted.

The psychoanalytic profession, however, abandoned Freud's bold theorizing and questioning. Against Freud's profound hopes, psychoanalysis became insular, medical, and clinical. It surrendered the general cultural terrain that Freud had staked out. Even the language of psychoanalysis came to reflect this surrender. To read almost any text by Freud is to enjoy a limpid and forthright style. Freud wrote simply and elegantly for a wide cultural audience. Much of Freud's greatness and impact, I believe, derives from this talent, the ability and wish to reach an educated public. Few recent American analysts have inherited either this capability or urge. In a technical and medical prose, contemporary analysts complacently write for one another.

In this book, I do not attribute this general abdication to a loss of talent; rather, I trace it to the cumulative effect of exile, professionalization, and Americanization, which prompted analysts to retreat both from public issues and a public forum. The first generations of analysts embraced psychoanalysis with a missionary zeal; they sought to reform the world or, at least, its sexual and social codes. They were rebellious intellectuals with broad cultural and political commitments. The spirit and ethos that animated them and their psychoanalysis did not endure.

The onset of nazism marked a break in psychoanalysis. Expelled from continental Europe, psychoanalysis shifted primarily to England and the United States. Psychoanalysis prospered in its new quarters; however, its very success hid the discontinuities, perhaps even defeats. The cultural and political spirit of classical analysis vaporized. In the course of its decades in America, psychoanalysis became in myth, and almost in fact, little more than an affluent medical specialty with an affluent clientele. By the 1950s few remembered how many of the early analysts were rebels or radicals or, simply, maverick intellectuals and humanitarians.

I survey the repression of psychoanalysis by way of the political Freudians of the second generation. The analysts of this generation were born at the turn of the century and were in the middle of their careers when fascism forced them into exile. They straddled two worlds: the world of classical psychoanalysis that flourished in the 1920s and 1930s, and that of an American psychoanalysis that matured in the 1940s and 1950s. Consequently, the transformation of psychoanalysis—its theoretical retreat—is etched in the lives of these analysts; and insofar as their project required living contact with a classical tradition, the fate of the political Freudians testifies to the general fate of psychoanalysis.

I should clarify that I do not believe for an instant that the immigrant analysts were hapless victims of a vulgar American culture. They were grateful—more than grateful—to live their lives and pursue their profession. They were victims of fascism, not of American culture. Nevertheless, in their new homes, many assumed a reserve about their nonconformist ideas; and this caution facilitated, rather than caused, a constriction in the collective psychoanalytic vision.

This book will follow the rise and fall of the political Freudians from Otto Gross in bohemian Munich before World War I to Robert Lindner in McCarthyite America, the first and last of a tradition. Between these figures, I situate Otto Fenichel and his circle. I hope to reclaim the political Freudians, and a classical tradition that sustained them, from the historical unconscious, and perhaps free psychoanalysis from its own repressions.

Los Angeles, California
January 1983

# ACKNOWLEDGMENTS

DURING the years that I sifted through the lives of the political Freudians I have incurred many personal debts to family, to friends, and to those who offered essential materials and memories. First of all I wish to thank Randi Markowitz for her support and generosity; in assembling and sharing with me Otto Fenichel's papers she made possible this study. For their warm encouragement and interest I would especially like to thank Norman Reider, Martin Grotjahn, Edith Ludowyk Gyömröi, and Clare Fenichel. I should note that while some principals in this study, or their families, have graciously responded to my questions, they have not read the manuscript and are not responsible for its contents. I should also record that both Dr. K. R. Eissler, secretary of the Sigmund Freud Archives, and Dr. Lore Reich Rubin refused to cooperate with my study; both possess materials by Fenichel that would have greatly facilitated my research. Others, however, have been of decisive help. I am grateful to: Kathleen Juline, librarian of the Los Angeles Psychoanalytic Society and Institute; the Hanna Fenichel Testamentary Trust for permission to quote from Otto Fenichel's unpublished writings; the John Simon Guggenheim Memorial Foundation for its support during a very lean period; and David James Fisher and Martin Shapiro for their comments and suggestions. For Naomi Glauberman, a consummate editor, and Sarah, our consummate daughter, thanks do not suffice: they have not let me forget what life is all about.

The Repression of Psychoanalysis

# CHAPTER ONE

# The Repression of Psychoanalysis

ON SATURDAY, 12 March 1938, Sigmund Freud jotted in his diary "Finis Austriae" as the Nazis marched into Vienna.[1] The next day, with England and France grumbling but passive, Austria officially ceased to exist. Ernest Jones hurriedly flew from London to help rescue Freud and found the streets full of "roaring tanks" and "roaring people."[2] On Tuesday, 15 March, an enthusiastic crowd crying "Sieg Heil!" drowned out the Führer himself as he addressed Vienna. Within two weeks the first transports carrying Austrians arrived at the Dachau concentration camp.[3]

Aided by a wide network, including President Roosevelt, Freud obtained permission to emigrate. The ailing doctor boarded the Orient Express which carried him to Paris, and from Paris he proceeded to London. As a final condition for his release, the Gestapo demanded that Freud sign a prepared statement affirming that he had been well treated. He signed, appending the ironic sentence, "I can heartily recommend the

Gestapo to anyone."[4] Although the Nazis had entered Freud's residence, looted his safe, and detained his daughter Anna, Jones still had to convince Freud to flee. He was very reluctant to abandon Vienna, his home for seventy-nine years. By contrast, for the analysts located in Germany, Hitler's rise to power five years earlier constituted a compelling argument for departing; they left for the major cities of the world from Paris to Prague to New York.

Nazism severed the psychoanalytic continuum. Psychoanalysis eventually prospered in exile, especially in the United States, but it never recaptured its original ethos and scope. When the refugees arrived they found a healthy psychoanalytic profession on the periphery of American cultural life. The refugees infused it with their own drive and ambition, but its orientation had shifted. The popular images of psychoanalysts as brainy Europeans with Teutonic accents had a factual basis. The major figures of American psychoanalysis from Erik Erikson to Erich Fromm, Heinz Hartmann, and Ernst Kris have been almost exclusively European refugees from fascism.

These figures belong to the second generation of analysts. The first generation was born in the 1870s and 1880s, and included Karl Abraham (1877), Sandor Ferenczi (1873), Max Eitingon (1881), Ernest Jones (1879), and Carl Jung (1875). By the 1930s, their work, if not completed, was set; its main lines were established. The members of the second generation were born around 1900; they were in their thirties and at a critical point in their lives when fascism intervened. They became refugees, petitioning unconcerned diplomats for visas and entry permits. Cut off from their past, thrown into new cultures, they were forced to reevaluate and redeploy their intellectual energies.

This second generation of analysts lived in two worlds, European and American. As they settled in cities such as New York and Chicago they attempted to re-create the milieu of Vienna or Berlin. They taught from the same texts they used in Europe and they organized seminars and institutes based on European models. They were successful—to a point. If they retained their expertise and training, they also abandoned much of psychoanalysis as they fled Europe.

What they left behind might be called the "culture" of psychoanalysis: the plans, projects, and spirit that imbued the discipline in its classic phase. Psychoanalysis in Europe was almost unthinkable without this culture; it permeated not only the texts, but also the lives of the early analysts. This virtually spiritual atmosphere, however, did not travel well; it hardly made an impression on American psychoanalysis. For this reason, it is news to American students that a radical, bohemian, and political ethos commonly pervaded European psychoanalysis. Few hints of the culture that prevailed in Vienna and Berlin remain in American psychoanalysis.

The refugee analysts settled in the United States in the 1930s. However, it was not until the 1950s, after the depression and the Second World War, that the public at large could turn its attention to psychoanalysis. Then psychoanalysis seemed very much in tune with the conservative and conformist times. It had become a respectable medical activity with prosperous practitioners and prosperous clients. As a theory or activity, it did not offer any particularly challenging social or political judgments. Rather, it appeared to be a fashionable treatment for fashionable ailments. As a discipline, it also seemed scientifically to confirm stereotypes of female and male roles.

In the course of thirty years from the Berlin of the 1920s to New York in the 1950s, psychoanalysis became transformed, and transformed itself. The second generation of analysts witnessed, suffered, and abetted this reconstruction of psychoanalysis; however, they only talked, often regretfully, among themselves about it. A grasp, even an inkling, of this change did not pass into the general culture. None of the second generation analysts publicly expressed a belief that the sleek American psychoanalysis did scant justice to the original project. Oddly, while the knowledge of Freud steadly increases, knowledge of the psychoanalytic movement and its original imperatives recedes.

Perhaps this is not so odd. Events within living memory are less secure than more distant happenings. Industrial society undermines an oral tradition. No one is expected to know by direct or indirect account the events of a century ago; they are learned through books and schools—or not at all. As we approach the present, where the written accounts do not (yet) exist, the role of living participants and witnesses increases, along with the risk of imperfect communication. Participants may not communicate their full knowledge for many reasons: they may, for example, think what they know is too obvious, the common coin of their generation; they may find the subject unpleasant; or they may lack an appropriate audience.

Consequently, a living knowledge of a culture may rapidly fade. Familiar insights of one generation may become totally lost to the next. What was known and immediate to the second generation of analysts may be unknown to the third and subsequent generations. These later generations have no way of learning that the second generation grew up within a radical political culture; that its members saw themselves as dissenters, pioneers, and cosmopolitan humanitarians. The second generation viewed psychoanalysis not only as a therapy but also as part of a larger social project. Yet they witnessed, and partly facilitated, the emergence of a narrowed psychoanalysis, an almost decultured, streamlined version.

To be sure, the newer generations of analysts and students have read and consulted the texts of the second generation, particularly the works of Otto Fenichel, Edith Jacobson, and Annie Reich. Indeed, these writings are deemed essential to the study of psychoanalysis. Thirty years after their initial publication, Fenichel's own essays, in his two-volume *Collected Papers*, are still in print; and, apart from Freud's own texts, perhaps no book shows up as frequently in psychoanalytic courses as Fenichel's *The Psychoanalytic Theory of Neurosis*. It has reached the status of "standard," an absolutely reliable benchmark of classical psychoanalytic information. A recent survey states that it is "justly" considered to "summarize all major psychoanalytic knowledge to that date."[5]

Nevertheless, these texts do not reveal that Fenichel or Jacobson or Annie Reich were not merely outstanding theorists and clinicians, they were also radicals devoted to a social psychoanalysis. This is not gossip or trivia; rather these convictions structured their lives. Moreover, they were not exceptions; many from their generation shared their commitments. Nevertheless this psychoanalytic culture, even a memory of it, did not survive the catastrophe of nazism. The psychoanalytic texts endured, but the spirit and culture vaporized. Americans who did not experience the European chapter accepted a reduced psychoanalysis, devoid of its politics and culture, as the whole enterprise.

For the refugees, suppression of their culture was a small price to pay. Initially they buried, adjourned or abandoned a political psychoanalysis in the name of personal survival. Fenichel spelled it out quite clearly several weeks after the Nazi invasion of Austria. Fenichel was then living in Prague. Like many analysts in Czechoslovakia, he had left Berlin in 1933 when the Nazis came to power. With Austria now part of the Reich, and with the prime minister of Britain, Neville Chamberlain, still making concessions—in the name of appeasement —to avoid war, the future of Czechoslovakian and European psychoanalysis looked dim. Fenichel knew that time was running out, and he prepared to abandon Europe.

Fenichel delivered a parting address to the Prague analysts in which he told the beleaguered group that a friend, who was not an analyst, had asked him to identify the pressing question in current psychoanalytic research. "I answered him: 'The question of whether the Nazis come to power in Vienna.' Now they have come." Fenichel's remarks to the Czechoslovakian group outlined the desperate situation facing psychoanalysis in 1938. The gathering barbarism imperiled all culture. For years, Fenichel stated, he had devoted himself to a psychoanalysis that was more than a private therapy; he had worked to develop a social and political theory. Now, these efforts belonged to history: "What once was is past." He felt that the overwhelming danger to life and liberty compelled theoretical modesty. The past hopes and plans had lost their urgency, even reality. "Many are oppressed; many are in need; and whoever thinks is threatened." A political psychoanalysis was no longer possible; survival itself was the watchword. The best one could do, Fenichel believed, was to preserve psychoanalysis and wait. The task was to "hold out" *(durchzuhalten)* (XLVIII /25 June, 1938/19).*

Fenichel spoke openly to the Prague group; he often employed the first person plural: "our hopes" and "our plans." He addressed friends, and more than friends, analysts who shared his devotion to a political, perhaps Marxist, psychoanalysis. The group included Annie Reich, Henry Lowenfeld, Steff Bornstein, and several others. Edith Jacobson briefly joined the Prague analysts before departing for New York. Each represented a common species, psychoanalysts with political and cultural commitments.

These names hardly account for all the political psychoanalysts of the second generation. The psychoanalytic mi-

---

*These parenthetical notations refer to Fenichel's unpublished *Rundbriefe* ("round letters"), which are cited throughout this book by letter number/date/section number. Letter numbers will be in Roman or Arabic in accord with Fenichel's own citations. The date of a letter indicates when the letter was circulated, not necessarily when its contents—an anthology of materials—were written or delivered. For instance, Fenichel made these remarks on 29 April 1938.

gration was already well advanced by 1938 and analysts were scattered across the globe. Psychoanalysis has treated them ambivalently. Many, including Siegfried Bernfeld and Otto Fenichel, remain familiar figures. Their oeuvre, however, survives laundered, its political and cultural vitality bleached out. The familiarity with their work is deceptive.

Familiarity, derived from family, implies a lengthy and close relationship; by virtue of its completeness, familiarity does not encourage further exploration. The familiar is well-charted, harboring no secrets or surprises. The major writings of Fenichel or Jacobson or Annie Reich are available; their contributions seem both solid and transparent, with neither shadows nor dark recesses; their writings can be summarized, studied, and categorized.

As psychoanalysts should know, however, the familiar is not outside history; it is drenched in the past. The familiar has been made familiar by effacing the foreign and, perhaps, forbidden; in this sense, psychoanalysts are acceptable after their unacceptable past has been censored. In brief, the lives and oeuvres of Fenichel and a wide group of other political analysts have been sanitized and prettified, often with their own cooperation. The catastrophe of exile and their ineluctable Americanization buried their nonconformist theories, hopes, and commitments. In the end, they fit in and succeeded by sacrificing their own identities.

The significance of the political Freudians transcends their own lives and contributions. The retrieval of Fenichel and other Freudians is only part of the story; the real story, and the real issue, is the nature of the psychoanalytic enterprise. The fate of the political Freudians points to and exemplifies a decisive turn in American psychoanalysis; that is, its palpable retreat from the cultural and political commitments that animated the early analysts, including Freud. The political Freudians are artifacts from a psychoanalytic dig; they summon up a village and culture of great vitality that has been paved over by the psychoanalytic highways of America.

It is important to realize that the Freudians of the first and second generation were primarily cosmopolitan intellectuals, not narrow medical therapists. Compared to recent American analysts, they represent another species. To Freud or Ferenczi or Jones, clinical practice did not exhaust psychoanalysis. Actively engaged with cultural and social issues, they spun audacious theories. The soundness of these theories—from Freud's *Totem and Taboo* to Ferenczi's *Thalassa*—is not the point; the theories testified to the reach and vitality of psychoanalysis in its classic period. The early analysts envisioned their science not only as a trade, but as a cultural and, sometimes, political force.

The number of these political Freudians was sizable and their individual contributions important. Most significant, however, was their collective devotion to social theorizing that kept alive the breadth of classical psychoanalysis; they were an index of the health of psychoanalysis. The political Freudians dissipated as classical psychoanalysis declined. When American psychoanalysis embraced a neutral clinical theorizing, it simultaneously became inhospitable to cultural and political psychoanalysis. The political Freudians, once common, became an extinct breed. To put it sharply, the repression of the political Freudians and the repression of psychoanalysis itself is the same story.

To recount this double tale of repression runs against the grain of contemporary psychoanalysis and, at the least, risks falling on deaf ears. The victory of the psychoanalytic establishment against its own dissenters—and ultimately against itself—harbors a self-perpetuating dynamic that is difficult to slow down or redirect. The political Freudians unsuccessfully resisted the intellectual division of labor which slices into modern cultural life. Psychoanalysis became what these analysts fought against, a medical specialty that relegated society to the sociologists, economics to the economists, and philosophy to the philosophers. Today few are less receptive to the political and cultural contours of psychoanalysis than professional analysts. This undermines in advance any attempts to reset the historical record. Even the appropriate vocabulary—"left-wing Freudians," "Marxist psychoanalysts," "political psychoanalysts," even "humanism" itself—sticks in the throat of contemporary psychoanalysis. These words today seem odd and foreign.

Foreign is the opposite of familiar: it is tempting to turn psychoanalysis on itself, the psychoanalysis of psychoanalysis. Freud wrote a sparkling essay on the power of the uncanny. The "uncanny is in reality nothing new or foreign, but something familiar and old-established in the mind that has been estranged only by the process of repression."[6] Together with another statement by Freud, a clue to the fate of the political analytic tradition may be in reach: "The doctrine of repression is the foundation-stone on which the whole structure of psychoanalysis rests."[7] Freud did not intend a (Freudian) double entendre, but it is arguable that the structure of psychoanalysis is founded on repression—the repression of its own past. The history of the political Freudians has been blocked; occasionally it troubles the sleep of psychoanalysis.

Psychoanalysts guard the past of their discipline. Far beyond the boundaries of ethics and decency, they have closed archives for decades, even centuries. Some material in the Sigmund Freud Collection of the Library of Congress, which includes the papers of many analysts, is closed until the twenty-second century! What is there to hide? In the typical chronicle, biography, or obituary, the socialist past of many analysts is not mentioned. Fenichel's more political writings were carefully omitted from his *Collected Papers*, assembled after his death. Just as an individual may pay for an obsession with a loss of vitality, for psychoanalysis as a whole, the obsessive flight from its past drains its theoretical life.

Today it is easy to forget how many early psychoanalysts identified themselves as socialists and Marxists. They may even have constituted a majority of the analysts. They included Paul Federn, Helene Deutsch, Siegfried Bernfeld, Herman Nunberg, Annie and Wilhelm Reich, Edith Jacobson, Willi Hoffer, Martin Grotjahn, Karl Landauer, Bruno Bettelheim, Ernst Simmel, and Fenichel. Before the onset of fascism these analysts were not isolated individuals. Located in Vienna and Berlin in the politically charged atmosphere of the late 1920s and early 1930s, their lives and projects frequently overlapped.

It is also difficult to remember the number of women participating in the psychoanalytic movement. After a decade of feminist criticism, it has become conventional wisdom that psychoanalysis constituted the vanguard of the sexual counterrevolution. Nothing is further from the truth. Regardless of the relative accuracy (or inaccuracy) of Freud's theory of female sexuality, indisputably psychoanalysis breathed of a sexual enlightenment and emancipation especially germane to women; psychoanalysis viewed women as sexual beings. Freud left no doubt that his female patients—originally the bulk of his practice—suffered from repression, sexual ignorance and misinformation.

Since psychoanalysis challenged repressive codes and received knowledge, it attracted not only women but also radicals and bohemians of all types. Apart from traditional professions assigned to women, such as teaching and nursing, it is likely that no other profession counted among its ranks as many women as did psychoanalysis in its early years. These women were not quiet and demure; they frequently bucked family and tradition to study psychoanalysis; they also were often cultural and political radicals. With a single exception, Fenichel's circle of political psychoanalysts was exclusively female. Today Helene Deutsch may symbolize repressive psychoanalytic theorizing about women. Yet as a young woman she identified with female emancipation, rubbed shoulders with Rosa Luxemburg, and called "the revelation of socialism" a great influence on her life.[8]

While the plans, hopes, and sometimes the writings of the political Freudians have been washed away, it must not be supposed that they passively suffered history: the repression of psychoanalysis is also its self-repression. The political Freudians themselves often facilitated and intensified the repression; this is why it is so difficult to reassemble, even find, the pieces of the story. The best sources—the political Freudians themselves —turned silent. The catastrophe of fascism and exile compelled or, at least, encouraged them to bury their own histories. In the United States, a hostility to Marxism intimidated the immigrants; it forced radicals, especially radical refugees, to clean out their bookshelves and censor their pasts.

Of course the erasure is never complete. Devoted disciples and biographers have documented the life and work of Wilhelm Reich, for example. Other political Freudians, however, have not fared as well. Cognoscenti of the history of psychoanalysis who recall that Fenichel was once a radical might imagine his Marxism belonged exclusively to the 1930s, when it was excusable. A recent history of psychoanalysis reports that Fenichel and Reich once led a Marxist opposition within the official psychoanalytic organization, "but it soon collapsed. In 1934 Reich was expelled from the International [Psychoanalytic Association]; Fenichel altered his views."[9]

This is not accurate: Fenichel did not alter his views; he hid them. The realities of exile compounded by the conservatism of the psychoanalytic establishment forced the radicalism of Fenichel and an entire network of analysts underground. Within a generation the past was dislodged; few wanted to remember; even fewer knew about this tradition. The rupture was so complete that often new friends and family members of these analysts had barely an inkling of their radical pasts.

When Fenichel died, Ernst Simmel, a socialist psychoanalyst from Berlin, wrote an informed obituary; he was completely conversant with Fenichel's life and activities. More recent obituaries written about this generation of political analysts were authored by people who did not share the European phase of their subjects' lives; moreover, published sources of information are unavailable. Edith Jacobson's obituary, for instance, does not mention that she was a socialist or a participant in Fenichel's political circle.[10] A more knowledgeable obituary of Berta Bornstein explains the dearth of information about her by the fact that "she never talked to her friends about her past, her family and background."[11] Edith Jacobson herself in an obituary of Annie Reich commented that "few colleagues know much about her past."[12]

The personal success of many of these analysts of the second generation masked their cultural defeat. In their private practices they prospered; but their commitment to a public and political psychoanalysis vegetated, and they failed to attract new students and followers. Fenichel had counseled his friends to "hold out" for better days to pursue a political psychoanalysis. By the 1960s when the cultural atmosphere in the United States had changed, it was too late. Many of the political Freudians had died; those still active were not inclined to pick up where they had left off.

The repression of psychoanalysis condenses several features of psychoanalytic history into a single term. Perhaps this label is misleading insofar as it misrepresents psychoanalysis as a homogeneous structure. Rather, psychoanalysis breaks down into a number of professional groups with a small army of academics trailing or leading. There exists, for example, besides the original and official organization of Freud's followers—the

# The Repression of Psychoanalysis

International Psychoanalytic Association and its affiliate, the American Psychoanalytic Association—other groups of practicing analysts. And scholars from widely diverse fields tap psychoanalysis. Today, these include historians, anthropologists, and literary theorists.

Apart from the organizational split between the Freudians and neo-Freudians (among the latter, Karen Horney, Erich Fromm and Clara Thompson), the newer professional associations do not raise issues germane to this study. In any case the International Psychoanalytic Association and the American Psychoanalytic Association occupied, and sometimes preoccupied, the professional lives of Freudians; they remain the touchstone.

The flowering of psychoanalysis within the universities is another matter. At its best, it inadvertently confesses to a crisis of professional psychoanalysis. As a lively intellectual discourse, psychoanalysis flourishes the more distant it is from practicing analysts. To put it more emphatically, as the doctors drummed out of their trade a cultural and political psychoanalysis, it took refuge in university divisions of literature and history.

Yet the vitality, though not the quantity, of psychoanalysis within the university is partly an illusion. Passed through the academic wringer, psychoanalysis emerges limp and colorless. Academic psychoanalysis does not escape the spell that nowadays bewitches almost all academic thought; it is directed exclusively toward colleagues. In relinquishing a larger educated audience outside its own particular disciplines, academic thought also surrenders readability. The journals and monographs are produced to be cited, not read.

The unreadability of current psychoanalytic writing characterizes both the work of academics and psychiatrists; of course, it cuts across all professional disciplines, and it is frequently deplored. Yet it calls for more than a conventional and unconvincing protest. The opaque psychoanalytic texts register the contraction of a humanist study that once appealed to a wide intellectual class into a technical discipline. While this disintegration of writing skills has affected many fields, it is especially marked in psychoanalysis. To chart an erosion in style between the writings of Max Weber and Talcott Parsons might challenge the finest minds and sensibilities. A chasm, however, divides the prose of Freud and current analysts.

Few of the many studies of Freud suggest that his impact, and perhaps his genius, may have derived from the simplicity of his writing. Freud wrote elegantly for a cultured public. He never received a Nobel Prize for medicine; he did obtain a literary award, the Goethe Prize.[13] In acknowledgment of the cultural breadth of his work, Freud's students invited Thomas Mann to deliver a key address upon Freud's eightieth birthday.[14] These honors reflect Freud's intellectual milieu, that of a literate and heterogeneous community. His texts endure not merely because they contain the original presentations of psychoanalysis, but because of their prose. Even a text like *The Question of Lay Analysis*, which might seem a technical discourse, is a small gem of lucid writing.

The decline of its prose is not a cause of the repression of psychoanalysis, although it is a sign of its contraction into a medical specialty. As psychoanalysis transformed itself into a private club open only to medical doctors, its language and substance unavoidably shifted. Exclusively engaged with clinical practice, the doctors ignored the cultural and political implications of analysis. Texts such as Freud's "Why War?" or his *The Future of an Illusion* did not prompt elaboration by clinicians. With no premium placed on readability by a literate public, psychoanalytic literature approached the standard and cramped norm of medical communications.

A complete account of the causes underlying the American repression of psychoanalysis will not be offered here; this would require, among other efforts, an evaluation of the American optimism and pragmatism that colored the European import. Studies such as Nathan G. Hale, Jr.'s *Freud and the Americans* have begun to address this project.[15] My own intention, rather, is to shed light on the repression of psychoanalysis—its mechanisms and tolls—by attending to the political Freudians.

The forces acting on psychoanalysis that are directly relevant to the political Freudians include professionalization and medicalization; the insecurity of immigrant analysts; hostility toward Marxism; and the impact of the neo-Freudians. Together these factors almost conspired to domesticate psychoanalysis, subduing its broader and also critical implications.

The exclusion of lay or nonmedical analysts accelerated, almost defined, the professionalization of psychoanalysis. Freud never doubted that the stakes were high in the feud over lay analysis: the preservation of psychoanalysis as a cultural force versus its contraction into a medical therapy. Standard references to Freud's supine followers conveniently forget that on this issue Freud's students almost universally rebuffed their master. Freud deployed all his power to defend nonmedical analysts; everywhere, especially in the United States, he encountered rebellion. American psychoanalysis virtually prohibited lay analysis.

As Freud feared, the elimination of lay analysis surrendered psychoanalysis to the medical doctors who reduced it to a recondite therapy. Several dire consequences followed. The medical imprint deeply penetrated the institutional, intellectual, and finally human bases of psychoanalysis. Psychoanalytic institutes and education subordinated themselves to medical imperatives. Insofar as medical doctors taught psychoanalysis to medical students, its more cultural dimensions were not censored, but slighted. "Medicalization exacted its price," Nathan G. Hale, Jr., writes, surveying the trajectory of American psychoanalysis. "Institute training was narrower than in Europe, and the rather broadly humanist culture of Berlin and Vienna did not survive well in the American medical air."[16] Perhaps the impact of medicalization on those who practice and write about analysis proved most damaging. Although it would be difficult to measure this impact with any precision, the accumulated testimonies and impressions suggest a fundamental change in the kind of individuals who are drawn to psychoanalysis. Even within the limits of medicine, European doctors have tended to be more cultured than their American counterparts; European medical education reflects, and partly causes, this richer humanist vision. American physicians obtain a more specialized education. With a lucrative renumeration as the reward, a technical education as the vehicle, and a keen competition to gain entry into medical school, the profession filters out mavericks, humanists, and dissenters.

Inasmuch as lay analysis has been eliminated, American physicians constitute the exclusive pool for psychoanalytic recruitment; obviously the doctors form psychoanalysis in their own image. Even many analysts have observed that, compared to the first and second generation of Europeans, the more recent American analysts were conventional and conservative; this shift in the human bases of the profession has profoundly affected psychoanalysis as a cultural and social theory.

Medicalization has also operated to limit the entry of women into the field of psychoanalysis. While in Europe the number of female analysts has been considerable, in the United States medicine has been almost exclusively a male preserve. Until very recently the United States had the dubious distinction of having among the lowest proportions of female physicians in the world, far below the average in Europe. Inasmuch as the medical community in the United States has supplied the candidates for psychoanalysis, few female doctors were even available. Consequently, only a limited number of women have navigated the American medical profession to become psychiatrists. Even today, many—perhaps most—of the female analysts are immigrants.

The nervousness and caution of the immigrant analysts themselves also facilitated the domestication of their discipline. Often the refugee analysts arrived in the United States after several stops; for instance, Fenichel fled from Berlin to Oslo to Prague and to Los Angeles within a five-year period. These immigrants knew only too well that the Western democracies were not rushing to open their doors to the victims of nazism. Those who gained entry into the United States were both grateful and understandably fearful of jeopardizing their tenuous legal status. They generally desired social and political invisibility, which in turn prompted a public conformism to prevailing intellectual trends. The insecurity of the refugees accelerated the Americanization of psychoanalysis.

Analysts with political pasts were especially cautious; they had participated in Austrian or German political life when socialism and Marxism were respectable theories and choices. It must be recalled that in central Europe the Communist parties did not monopolize Marxism. Huge Social Democratic parties in Austria and Germany also made claim to Marxism, and these Social Democratic parties were almost popular institutions, deeply rooted in public life. To be sure, compared to the Communist parties, the Social Democrats were hardly subversive. Robert Michels's classic work on bureacratic conservatism, *Political Parties*, dwells on the German Social Democracy as its prime case.[17]

Nevertheless the Social Democrats appealed to the legacy of Marx. In Austria, especially, Social Democracy brought forth a number of distinguished theorists, among them, Otto Bauer, Karl Renner, and Rudolf Hilferding. Many, perhaps even a majority of European analysts, were themselves Social Democrats; personal associations between analysts and Social Democrats were close. Freud himself was linked to the socialists in a number of ways.[18]

There is a letter of Freud's that highlights not only his proximity to the Austrian Social Democrats, but also the distorted way—minor though illustrative—in which this information was transmitted to later American analysts. In 1956 the psychoanalyst Martin Grotjahn, himself the son of a prominent Berlin Social Democrat, Alfred Grotjahn, published in the official American psychoanalytic journal a letter Freud wrote to Julie Braun-Vogelstein. Her husband, Heinrich Braun, a student friend of Freud's, had died, and she wrote to Freud in 1927 asking for his reminiscences about her husband. He responded in part:

The last impressive meeting which we had may have taken place in 1883 (?) or 1884 (?). He came to Vienna then and invited me for lunch at his brother-in-law's, Victor Adler. I still remember that he was a vegetarian then and that I had a chance to see the little Fritz who must have been one or two years of age. (I think it is remarkable that this happened in the same rooms in which I have been living for thirty-six years.)[19]

In his commentary, Grotjahn, who certainly knew all the facts, noted vaguely that Heinrich Braun was an editor and "leader in the theory of social economy and its political applications"; and that Victor Adler was a "physician, psychiatrist and political leader in Vienna. Victor Adler and Heinrich Braun shared the same political philosophy."[20] In 1956—the year the Hungarian revolt was put down by the Soviet army—Grotjahn was writing very carefully. His phrases—"leader in the theory of social economy," "shared the same political philosophy"— managed to avoid stating the obvious: Braun and Adler were the most prominent socialists of the day. Braun edited the main Social Democratic theoretical journals, and Adler was chairman of the party. Nor did Grotjahn indicate that "little

Fritz" grew up to be a "political assassin," to use the subtitle of a recent biography. In the third year of World War I, Friedrich Adler shot the prime minister of Austria shouting "Down with tyranny! We want peace!"[21] Nor does this exhaust the interest of the letter. As Freud indicated to Julie Braun-Vogelstein, he was living in the rooms where he had originally met her husband and Adler. The fact tht Freud purchased Adler's home, the famous Berggasse 19, and lived in it for most of his life, has been suggestive to several historians. They have surmised that Freud wished to supplant the revolutionary leader, who had overshadowed him when they had been students together.[22]

The tangled web of psychoanalysis and socialism—personal and theoretical—unraveled in the United States. The refugee analysts realized that they had entered a terrain very different from that of Central Europe. Even if the 1930s was a high-water mark for American Marxism, it never gained the prestige or acceptance of European Social Democracy. Marxism and socialism remained culturally marginal in the United States, if not suspect—especially among conservative doctors. The immigrant analysts therefore tabled their political beliefs and nonconformist opinions in order to ease their integration into American life. In Berlin, Ernst Simmel had been president of the Berlin Psychoanalytic Institute; he had also presided over the Association of Socialist Physicians. In the United States his connection to socialist groups ceased. Fenichel believed his own political past slowed his naturalization. For those who did not get the message postwar McCarthyism made it clear.

The issue in the United States was not the persecution of dissidents and intellectuals, but the insecurity of political refugees who were legal aliens; understandably, to avoid attention, they assumed the lowest possible political profile. Even on narrower organizational and theoretical issues facing American psychoanalysis, they were cautious. Fenichel often reiterated that he did not want himself and his collaborators to appear as a clique of immigrants who in accented English opposed the main thrust of American psychoanalysis.

The immigrant analysts infused vast energy into psychoanalysis, but in splitting off their political and cultural commitments they abetted its Americanization. Of course, this process was not obvious to them at the time. Fenichel secretly worked to sustain an opposition in the hope that the climate in the American psychoanalytic community would allow a more public identity. However, the situation did not change, and the opposition remained secret until it finally disappeared. Although a body of dissenting literature, ideas, and programs survived, the disciples and successors to develop these did not materialize. Why?

The transmission of knowledge across generations is more delicate than one would suppose. To remain a vital force, knowledge, especially psychoanalytic knowledge, requires the living contact of teachers and students. Knowledge is bathed in emotions, desires, and commitments. Without these nurturing fluids, it withers into empty words. Texts can be saved and studied, but they lose their urgency; they drift out of the public culture to library shelves. This fate befell political psychoanalysis, and indeed much of classical psychoanalysis. On the basis of their own commitments, the political Freudians did not seek or attract students; nor did they impart the full body of their ideas to the students they did have. Within a single generation, their ideas came to be completely excluded from mainstream psychoanalysis. The newer generation of analysts, essentially devoted to clinical issues and practice, lacked living contact with the breadth of psychoanalysis. By the 1950s, the very few psychoanalytic rebels, such as Robert Lindner, were theoretically stranded; classical analysis was only a memory to a few refugees.

The critical role of the neo-Freudians in facilitating the

# The Repression of Psychoanalysis

Americanization of psychoanalysis is difficult to assess. I pursued the subject briefly in chapters 5 and 7, and it has been discussed elsewhere by numerous commentators. To Fenichel and his circle, the neo-Freudians exemplified Americanization; they watered down a radical depth psychology that hinted of liberation into a tepid doctrine of social meliorism. Nevertheless, Fenichel shared with the neo-Freudians a dissatisfaction with the conservatism of "establishment" psychoanalysis in America. The political Freudians were paralyzed by their half-solidarity with and half-antagonism toward the neo-Freudians.

Two opposite tendencies in the process of Americanization fed off of each other. On the one hand, a secure orthodoxy embraced the medical establishment and dispensed with the culture and humanism of classical psychoanalysis. On the other hand, the neo-Freudians managed to salvage this culture but at the cost of jettisoning the erotic and unconscious dimensions of psychoanalysis. The neo-Freudians also successfully filled the public space that the orthodox analysts had vacated as they evolved into clinicians. Offering accessible books, the neo-Freudians oriented themselves toward a wider public.

The repression of psychoanalysis proceeded by these two contradictory routes, medical professionalization and theoretical banalization. Neither the orthodox nor the revisionist analysts preserved the scope and ambition of classical analysis; rather a constricted medical version confronted a flat cultural version. It is important to grasp that these two tendencies fostered each other. Unhappiness with an obdurate medical orthodoxy spurred rebellions that yielded a thin neo-Freudianism; and unhappiness with a popular neo-Freudian moralizing prolonged the grasp of a conservative orthodoxy.

Political Freudians sought to remain loyal both to the depth dimensions of psychoanalysis—its unconscious and erotic levels—and to its humanist implications. If theoretically cogent, practically and organizationally the political Freudians were defeated. On the institutional battlefield of American analysis, only two sides mustered sizable forces: orthodox and revisionist. The political Freudians sympathized with the cultural and social impulse of the neo-Freudians, but they could not subscribe to a doctrine that radically abridged psychoanalysis; they sympathized with the loyalty of the orthodox analysts to classical psychoanalysis but profoundly objected to their social and political blindness. In effect the political Freudians were homeless.

The fate of Fenichel perfectly illustrates the repression of psychoanalysis. For countless students and professionals Fenichel is synonymous with his *Psychoanalytic Theory of Neurosis;* and this text is regarded as synonymous with reliable and comprehensive psychoanalytic knowledge. It also seems conservative to a fault. A review in the progressive journal, *The New Republic,* complains that the book ducks the social reality, concluding it often "runs against social facts; but they are hardly ever acknowledged as such and are never elaborated."[23]

Ironically, little animated Fenichel more than the "social facts" of psychoanalysis. Today, this is hardly obvious, for, to the uninitiated, Fenichel exemplifies establishment psychoanalysis—and for good reason. In exile, he hid but did not renounce his political vision of psychoanalysis; indeed, Fenichel pursued his political theorizing but outside of a public forum. Nor was he alone; many refugee analysts publicly represented an almost neutral psychoanalysis while privately they remained steadfast in their devotion to its social and political implications.

Fenichel stood at the hub of these analysts. As he was completing *The Psychoanalytic Theory of Neurosis,* he was also relinquishing his leadership of a secret group of political analysts. The story of this circle constitutes a veritable repressed chapter of psychoanalytic history: at the heart of the analytic establishment some of the most prominent practitioners sustained a secret and dissenting network.

For almost twelve years, beginning in Berlin where they had all assembled, Fenichel assiduously, almost fanatically, directed this group. As exile dispersed them, Fenichel maintained contact by a regular system of *Rundbriefe* ("round letters"). The group was secret. Fenichel often advised them to destroy the letters, which most of them did; consequently, few copies exist today. Fenichel and six other analysts composed the core group. Fenichel, Edith Jacobson, and Annie Reich are the best known of the circle; Kate Friedländer is known in England; and Barbara Lantos, Edith Ludowyk Gyömröi, and George Gero are the least prominent. (It is possible that Berta Bornstein also belonged to the group.)

They shared an almost identical cultural background; in this respect they accurately represented the first generations of analysts. Bruno Bettelheim, an acquaintance of Fenichel's, wrote recently of his own past: "As a child born [1903] into a middle class assimilated Jewish family in Vienna, I was raised and educated in an environment that was in many respects identical with the one that had formed Freud's background."[24] Although not all were Viennese, those in Fenichel's circle all belonged to the secure bourgeoisie of central Europe.

Members of the circle were also close in age; their birthdates clustered around 1900: Fenichel, 1897; Edith Jacobson, 1897; Annie Reich, 1902; Kate Friedländer, 1903; George Gero, 1901; Barbara Lantos, 1894; Edith Ludowyk Gyömröi, 1896; and Berta Bornstein, 1899. The dates themselves suggest a critical distance from Freud. His world was rapidly succumbing to the ravages of war, revolution, and economic depression. The members of Fenichel's group were all in their teens and early twenties when World War I and the postwar revolutions resolutely ended the nineteenth century.

Perhaps the first reference to Fenichel in the psychoanalytic literature appears in the *Minutes of the Vienna Society*. Siegfried Bernfeld, already well known as a leader of socialist youth, lectured the Society on Poetic Writing by Youth. The ensuing discussion included a comment by a "guest" identified as "medical student Fenichel."[25] Fenichel was just twenty. This discussion took place in the middle of the events that molded the lives of the political Freudians. At the time of this meeting of the Vienna Society (19 November 1918) World War I had been over for a week. The Provisional National Assembly in Vienna ended six centuries of the Austro-Hungarian Monarchy by declaring a republic some days earlier. The Bolsheviks, celebrating the first birthday of the Russian Revolution, faced Europe, expecting and promoting revolution. Throughout Germany and Austria workers and soldiers returned from the fronts to form self-governing councils. In the next weeks and months, Soviet republics were established in Budapest and Munich. The Spartacists called for revolution in Berlin; right-wing military outfits galvanized; political assassinations became regular events; Rosa Luxemburg was murdered.

These events resonated throughout the lives of Fenichel and his friends. Fenichel, Annie Reich, and Edith Jacobson participated in the left and Jewish youth movements that swept Germany and Austria in the first decades of the century. The Hungarians (Lantos, Gero, and Gyömröi) moved in the Budapest student circles around George Lukács and Karl Mannheim. Lukács assumed the position of cultural commissar in the brief Hungarian Revolution of 1919 and went on to become one of Europe's most prominent Marxists.[26] Mannheim, an equally prominent sociologist, remained a socialist (and critic of Marxism); his wife, Julia Mannheim, became a psychoanalyst.[27]

The careers of the political Freudians followed roughly parallel courses. In the years 1915–20 they engaged in left-wing political activities—student and youth politics. In the early

1920s, they completed medical degrees and analytic training and went on to establish practices; political commitments became subordinated to professional work. In the later 1920s the conflict among Social Democrats, Communists, and Nazis charged the political and cultural atmosphere of Weimar Germany. These Freudians became drawn not simply to politics but to the project of a political psychoanalysis.

They all gravitated to Berlin. Otto Friedrich explains:

Marlene Dietrich, Greta Garbo, Josephine Baker, the grandiose productions of Max Reinhardt's "Theatre of the 5,000," three opera companies running simultaneously . . . the opening night of *Wozzeck*, and *The Three Penny Opera*. . . . Almost overnight the somewhat staid capital of Kaiser Wilhelm had become the center of Europe, attracting scientists like Einstein and von Neumann, writers like Auden and Isherwood, the builders and designers of the Bauhaus School. . . . Above all, Berlin in the 1920s represented a state of mind, a sense of freedom and exhilaration.[28]

It also attracted the leftist analysts. By 1930 the participants in Fenichel's circle all resided in Berlin.[29] Several joined the Communist party. A veritable garden of left-wing analytic groups emerged.

By 1933, when Hitler attained power, it was over. Jewish Marxist psychoanalysts were thrice marked—as Jews, Marxists, and psychoanalysts—and were eager to exit. Martin Grotjahn recalls helping Ernst Simmel out his back window when Simmel received a message that the Nazis were en route to arrest him.[30] Fenichel fled to Oslo, Prague, and then to the United States. Gero departed first for Copenhagen and later America. Annie Reich moved to Prague and afterward New York. Friedländer and Lantos first settled in Paris and later London. Gymöröi spent some years in Budapest before immigrating to Ceylon. Jacobson lingered in Germany and was arrested; she later escaped to New York. A chapter in psychoanalysis closed.

27

Not quite. As the analysts dispersed, Fenichel commenced the *Rundbriefe;* he sought to keep alive a left-wing analytic tradition. At times he considered the letters a "written" extension of a seminar his group had all frequented in Berlin. Privately and cautiously he hoped these analysts would continue to discuss the issues critical to a political psychoanalysis.

This was not the first secret grouping or system of *Rundbriefe* in the history of psychoanalysis. For a number of years Freud and "the committee" communicated by "round letters." In the wake of unsettling splits in the psychoanalytic movement, Ernest Jones had proposed that "we form a small group of trustworthy analysts as a sort of 'Old Guard' around Freud." Freud greeted the idea with joy: "What took hold of my imagination immediately is your idea of a secret council composed of the best and most trustworthy among our men to take care of the future development of psychoanalysis." Freud stressed, "First of all: This committee would have to be *strictly secret* in its existence and in its actions."[31] In addition to Freud six analysts originally composed "the committee": Rank, Abraham, Sachs, Eitingon, Ferenczi, and Jones. Between 1920 and 1924 the committee circulated round letters.[32]

Fenichel's group was also secret and was also composed of six members. Technically its members did not circulate round letters. Instead, Fenichel sent out identical letters to each member who in turn responded, commented, or amended the contents by writing directly to Fenichel. Fenichel then cited or summarized the responses in the next *Rundbrief.* This procedure facilitated and hastened the communication, since letters did not have to circulate slowly from one recipient to another with each adding comments. Rather, everything was directed to Fenichel, who organized, edited, and typed out the identical letters.

Few collections of correspondence equal Fenichel's *Rundbriefe;* and even to call them letters is misleading. Fenichel lavished unselfish energy on these communications. Not destined for publication or a wide public, they testified to a devotion to psychoanalytic theorizing that sought not recognition but mutual understanding. They were not casual or intermittent affairs. In the days before cheap photocopying, Fenichel typed out the letters with at least six carbons, and he carefully corrected the typing errors in each carbon. Each letter was numbered, and each was subdivided into numbered sections. There were a total of 119 letters extending over eleven and a half years.[33] His gargantuan effort concluded on 14 July 1945. His final letter explained that due to diminished involvement by the recipients the correspondence no longer merited his energies. Six months later Fenichel was dead.

These letters were not brief. Short ones might be ten pages; more frequently, they ran in the range of fifteen to twenty-five pages; and often they reached forty to sixty pages. The longest, almost eighty pages, was Fenichel's first communication from the United States, typed, as usual, with six carbons, each corrected. From Oslo, Prague, and Los Angeles Fenichel's letters came, informing, arguing, commenting, and reproducing incoming reports. Altogether they constitute perhaps some three thousand pages of manuscript or, if published unedited, four to five stout volumes.

Theoretical discussions and exchanges, their original purpose, formed the heart of the *Rundbriefe*. At first the group's relationship with Wilhelm Reich received considerable attention. Fenichel worked to elaborate "our" position, meaning that of the political analysts who did not follow Reich. Lengthy discussions on national character and the Oedipus complex meandered through many letters. These debates overlapped with exchanges that Fenichel first conducted privately, outside the *Rundbriefe*—for instance, with Erich Fromm or Abram Kardiner. He cited such exchanges wholesale in the *Rundbriefe* and invited responses.

THE REPRESSION OF PSYCHOANALYSIS

Fenichel's group tried to meet on more than one occasion; this was difficult because members were scattered across Europe. They often discussed their tactics, since Fenichel did not want them to appear publicly as a compact and tight organization. At the time of the Marienbad Psychoanalytic Congress Fenichel broached how they might gather without drawing attention to themselves. A suggestion to retreat to a hotel some miles away, where no one might stumble upon them, was debated. In fact, they succeeded in preserving their secrecy—to a fault. Few of their contemporaries, and fewer later analysts, learned of their existence.

While the literature on Wilhelm Reich and Erich Fromm, often based on their own autobiographical essays, continually grows, next to nothing has been written on Fenichel. Yet he shared with Reich and Fromm a common past that reached back to the same Berlin study group; the three constituted the most productive, committed, and original of the political Freudians. This neglect of Fenichel derives from his success in camouflaging his thought, especially significant because it was so typical of the political psychoanalysts. While Reich and Fromm departed from Freud, Fenichel's group remained committed to classical psychoanalysis. Their public orthodoxy and private heresies illuminate the subterranean history of psychoanalysis.

Fenichel initiated, sustained, and terminated the *Rundbriefe;* he was the force behind the group which, in fact, occasionally was called "Fenichel's circle," a term he did not like. It was a circle of kindred analysts; yet it was also a one-man show. The *Rundbriefe* served as the lifeline for a group in exile, but it was Fenichel who did the typing, editing, and lion's share of the writing. None of the others came close to expending in a year the time and effort that Fenichel devoted each month.

## The Repression of Psychoanalysis

Even as I follow the contours of his life, I do not intend to write Fenichel's biography or probe his emotional life. If psychoanalysis conducted in an office is fraught with difficulties, that conducted by way of incomplete letters and texts would vie for validity with astrology. In any case Fenichel's significance resides more in the psychoanalytic and political networks he established and represented. As a youth-movement activist, Jew, psychoanalyst, socialist, and refugee, Fenichel expressed the spirit of his times. I do not wish to imply that Fenichel was simply an exemplary product of his situation; however, I do wish to emphasize that the issue here is the fate of Fenichel's project and circle as well as of psychoanalysis as a whole.

Nevertheless, this story would be incomplete without at least some comments about Fenichel the person. The very difficulty of gaining access to his emotional life suggests the world of Freud; a sharp line divided the public and private person. The thousands of pages of *Rundbriefe* are almost completely impersonal. Fenichel arrived in New York as an immigrant, traveled across the continent, and settled in Los Angeles. The letter of close to eighty pages he sent out from Los Angeles contained hardly a word on his reactions to New York, the midwest, California, or American life. He reported only on the psychoanalytic situation in various cities. At the same time, over the course of his life, he vented his feelings in poems, which he apparently showed to no one.

Fenichel perfectly represented a culture that gave much to the world, the turn-of-the-century Jewish Viennese bourgeois family. Many of its sons and daughters shared a supreme self-discipline, devotion to learning, and introspection. A small library can be filled with studies of Jewish identity in the German-speaking countries of this period.[34] The Jews—especially those who, like Fenichel's father, were from Eastern Europe—were indebted to Germany for abolishing legal discrimination. They valued, prized, and finally identified with high German culture. In his youth Fenichel filled notebooks with poems by Rilke.

Those who knew Fenichel recalled his prodigious capacity for work, his photographic memory, and his razor-sharp intellect. Ralph R. Greenson's memoir of Fenichel is subtitled "The Encyclopedia of Psychoanalysis." The 1,600 bibliographical references in *The Psychoanalytic Theory of Neurosis*, Greenson reminded us, were not decorative; integrated into the text, they evidenced Fenichel's "enormous fund of knowledge and a fabulously retentive memory."[35] (And Greenson might not have been aware that Fenichel considered these references a poor substitute for the comprehensive bibliography he had prepared for the volume; a shortage of paper, due to the war, prevented its use.) Rudolph M. Lowenstein's obituary remembered Fenichel's "exceptional intelligence, his extraordinary memory and his unusual capacity for work."[36] Bertram Lewin characterized Fenichel as an "eager and alert intellect, an indefatiguable worker and student, an avid and incisive observer, digester, elaborator and systematizer."[37]

If only by its quantity, the published record supports these judgments. Fenichel's life was relatively short, forty-eight years, and the last thirteen were beset by the misfortunes of exile, not the least of which included the exhausting effort of moving and establishing legal status in several countries. Despite the turmoil, Fenichel's productivity remained awesome. The standard bibliography of his works runs some twenty pages and includes over five hundred items.[38] Without letup, Fenichel wrote essays, books, reviews, and abstracts. His published works—outside of the *Rundbriefe*—tower in quantity above the writings of the others in his circle. His second wife recalled that he would excuse himself after dinner and a half hour later would reappear to read her a complete paper from a series of paragraphs he had jotted down.[39] Others report that, at every spare moment, even between patients, Fenichel would type or take notes.

The discipline and dedication of Fenichel's generation are almost obsolete; they valued their own cultural education with unsurpassed seriousness. For instance, during the course of his life, Fenichel kept a list of every cultural production he attended. He would enter the details—name, author, date, place —in a regular Viennese artifact, a "Concert and Theater Book," advertised as essential for all those who take "seriously" art and "Geist." His parents kept track of his early cultural experiences, and he transcribed and maintained the list throughout his wanderings. The productions ran from *Frau Holle, Max and Moritz,* and *Hansel and Gretel* when Fenichel was four, five, and six years of age to the 392nd entry, *Oklahoma,* seen in New York in June 1945.

Fenichel was a man of lists. If nothing were known of his published works or the *Rundbriefe,* it would be difficult to believe that he did anything but list. He was consumed and inundated with lists. Everything he did was jotted down somewhere, often several places, and was then cross-listed, added up, charted, alphabetized, and numbered. Even the entries in his "Concert and Theater Book" were not simply enumerated; they were recategorized on separate sheets, evaluated, for example, by number of cultural events per year (a high of twenty-two in 1916 and a low of one in 1901 when he was only four!), or events per country (one in the USSR, two in Italy, and so on). He also listed and numbered every movie he saw (a total of 530), including the location of the cinema and his companions. He documented every train trip, no matter how minor, and by 1925, when the list apparently stops, he had cited over 800. Every auto excursion was listed, complete with destination, stopping points, and traveling companions; the last trip entered was number 859, Christmas 1945, to Palm Springs, California. There were scores of other lists, catalogs, and enumerations, often completely private and opaque, including—possibly—a list of the women he slept with.

Two lists dwarfed all others. On a fat wad of paper he kept a log, in shorthand, with one-line entries for every day, beginning in 1911 until the end of his life, and he kept a comprehensive catalog of his correspondence. He maintained an immense correspondence, receiving some ten thousand letters in his lifetime. Each incoming letter was assigned a number; next to the number he noted the author, date, and origin. A separate sheaf of papers listed authors alphabetically, and next to each author's name he added the number of the letter.

Fenichel's fondness for lists was probably complemented by his photographic memory. Among his friends it was well known that Fenichel possessed instant recall not only of passages from Freud (with page numbers), but of the entire European train schedule. His mental feats and discipline proved practical. The rigorous systematization of his correspondence enabled him to fetch with ease any letter. He brought the same zeal and logic to his research and reading; he noted, abstracted, and cataloged everything he read. When queried on a subject, he could retrieve within moments appropriate bibliographical information. On this solid foundation he built his books and essays.

Fenichel's incessant listing and enumerating should not mislead; it would be unfair to indulge in pop psychoanalytic notions of an anal or compulsive character. Nor should the element of play or games which informed his listing be ignored; he was regularly engaged in private competitions, for instance, counting the number of letters he received by city and country within a particular time period, presumably to discover the "winner."

All who knew him testify to his zest for living, his gusto for travel, and love of humor.[40] He was far from a dour systematizer. Like Freud, he was a witty conversationalist and connoisseur of Jewish jokes. He even mimicked himself and derided his own fondness for schedules and guidebooks. His humor and laughter are the first things his friends recall. He was also generous with his money, helping acquaintances and family.

His students found him not only a brilliant lecturer but also a good listener. An intense concentration on texts marked his seminars. Grotjahn recalled a Berlin seminar on Freud's analysis of the Schreber case that covered only two pages in a semester. Greenson described a seminar in Los Angeles that after three hours had not got beyond the word "libido" in the second sentence of the first essay in Freud's *Three Essays on Sexuality.* "Those evenings were so stimulating that . . . several of us continued the debate until well after midnight—on the sidewalk in front of Fenichel's house."[41] In an unpublished manuscript, Fenichel revealed his pedagogical thoroughness: "175 Topics of Discussion about Freud's *Three Contributions to the Theory of Sex* for the Use of Freud Seminars."

Fenichel never minced words; nor did he defer to anyone. Hence many found him oversharp and intolerant. His critical spirit was ruthlessly democratic. He listened to everyone; his seminars were open to all; and he bluntly differed with anyone, including Freud and senior analysts. Yet he seemed to bear no grudges; even though he railed against the general theories and influence of Sandor Rado and Franz Alexander —two of his bêtes noires—he appreciated occasional papers they wrote.

Otto Fenichel was a formidable person, intellect, and presence in psychoanalysis. As the *Rundbriefe* hint, Freud and the Viennese analysts deeply respected Fenichel and even feared him. Smarting from the "loss" of Wilhelm Reich, who in the 1920s was considered a wunderkind, they very much wanted to keep Fenichel within the psychoanalytic fold. They need not have worried. Fenichel gave his mind, heart, and life to psychoanalysis. We will never know, however, of what he was capable; he failed to husband his energies, and he died too young. Some forty years younger than Freud, he survived the master only by six years. Fenichel's chef d'oeuvre, *The Psychoanalytic Theory of Neurosis*, was published in December 1945, while he was celebrating his forty-eighth birthday. Within weeks, on 22 January 1946, as the letters still poured in with congratulations for the book, Fenichel died.

# CHAPTER TWO

# Spring's Awakening: Analysts as Rebels

MYTHS of the educated depict psychoanalysis as a reactionary force in a somnolent pre–World War I Europe. This assessment is inaccurate on two counts. A reforming zeal permeated early psychoanalysis; and its social environs reverberated with a cultural rebellion. The Utopian and revolutionary spirit often ascribed to the 1920s and the Weimar Republic more properly belonged to this earlier prewar period. Cubism, atonal music, Futurism, linguistic philosophy, as well as psychoanalysis flowered before the war. Many of these innovations, as T. W. Adorno observes, were already fading by the 1920s. "The heroic period of the new art lies much more around 1910."[1]

A revolt among the youth of Europe marked the prewar era and left its imprint on psychoanalysis. Throughout central Europe youth, often yearning to "return to nature" and a freer existence, fled the constrictions of bourgeois life. The themes of youth (and sons) against fathers and schools regularly surfaced in the contemporary literature. Even the titles of the works indicated the explosive tension: Walter Hasenclever's *Der Sohn* ("The Son"); Arnold Bronnen's *Vatermord* ("Parricide"); Frank Wedekind's *Spring's Awakening,* and Heinrich Mann's *Professor Unrat* (better known under its film title "The Blue Angel")—all tap the revolt of youthful sexuality. Many analysts of the second generation, Fenichel, Annie Reich, Siegfried Bernfeld, and Willi Hoffer, participated in the youth movement.

It is frequently forgotten (repressed?) that Freud himself championed a reform of sexual mores and codes. Particularly before the war, Freud often questioned the costs of excessive sexual repression; he even made a quiet claim to the mantle of emancipator of youth. Discussing his break with Carl Jung, Freud commented that the Zurich psychiatrist's renunciation of unconscious sexuality makes "it improbable from the start" that Jung's "revised version of psychoanalysis can justify claim to be a liberation of youth." Freud added, obviously alluding to himself: "In the last resort it is not the years of the doer that determines this [the liberation of youth] but the character of the deed."[2]

The character of Freud's deed is expressed in his " 'Civilized' Sexual Morality and Modern Nervousness" (1908), perhaps his most militant social work. The quotation marks around "civilized" indicate Freud's radical probing. "It is certainly not the physician's business to come forward with proposals for reform," he announced as he came forward with proposals for reform. He questions whether "our 'civilized' sexual morality is worth the sacrifice which it imposes upon us." And he measures its price with almost a Nietzschean eye; excessive sexual suppression yields "conciliatory and resigned" crowd followers: "I have not gained the impression that sexual abstinence helps to shape energetic, self-reliant men of action, nor original thinkers, bold pioneers and reformers; far more often it produces 'good' weaklings who later become lost in the crowd." Nor does he doubt that the burden falls most heavily on women, restricting them to "unappeased desire, infidelity or neurosis."[3]

The year (1909) following publication of this paper, Freud lectured in the United States, and to raised eyebrows he again advocated a freer sexual life. He closed his lectures with the reminder that sexuality requires some direct satisfaction: "Our civilized standards make life too difficult for the majority of human organizations. . . . We ought not to seek to alienate the whole amount of energy of the sexual instinct from its proper ends." He warned that the attempt to do this risked crippling or exhausting the individual. To illustrate the danger of excessive sexual repression, Freud closed his American lectures with a parable.

The citizens of a little German town, Schilda, possessed a remarkably strong horse, which, however, consumed a large quantity of expensive oats. To break this bad habit, each day they reduced its rations "till they had accustomed it to complete abstinence. For a time things went excellently: the horse was weaned to the point of eating only one stalk a day, and on the succeeding day it was at length to work without any oats at all. On the morning of that day the spiteful animal was found dead; and the citizens of Schilda could not make out what it had died of." Freud added that "we" think the animal starved to death.[4]

To be sure, Freud cannot be simply categorized as a cultural or sexual radical. Nevertheless a reforming and social impulse unmistakably ran through many of his texts. This impulse permeated the psychoanalytic movement, attracting and sustaining individuals unhappy with the sexual and social codes of the day. When, as young adults and students, the future analysts of the second generation bridled at social restrictions, Freud's reforming vigor was at its height. There was an obvious affinity between youthful rebellion and psychoanalysis.

It also had its limits. Freud skillfully juggled the conflicting imperatives of cultural rebel and political moderate. Personally Freud tolerated, even encouraged heretics and bold theoreticians; he often defended mavericks such as the "wild" analyst Georg Groddeck before his more respectable students. Yet Freud was not a cultural revolutionary, and when challenged by radical psychoanalysts he would retreat into the medical boundaries that he otherwise disdained. "We are doctors and wish to remain doctors."[5] With these words Freud flagged the psychoanalytic boundaries in his reproof of Otto Gross, a now forgotten rebel analyst.

Nevertheless, Freud's boundaries cut off a wide territory; in fact, for a historical moment, they even encompassed Otto Gross, who was very much a part of the life of both Freud and Jung. Gross (1887–1920) did not belong to the second generation of Freudian analysts; rather, he belonged to the analytic world on the eve of that generation's emergence. His ideas and activities captured an atmosphere, the vitality of classical psychoanalysis, which the next generation inhaled. In Gross, psychoanalysis encountered its first political and sexual rebel, a predecessor to Wilhelm Reich. For all his craziness, and perhaps because of it, Gross revealed a subversive psychoanalysis that the second generation inherited and systematized.

Otto Gross received public notoriety when, several months before the arrival of World War I, a story appeared in a Viennese newspaper headlined "Forced Internment of a Scholar in an Insane Asylum." Subtitled, "Professor Hans Gross against His Son," the story read in part:

The famed criminologist Dr. Hans Gross had his son, Dr. Otto Gross, a successful and active Berlin researcher in the field of psychoanalysis, seized and incarcerated in an Austrian insane asylum. The seizing of Dr. Gross was well prepared and rapidly executed. One day three powerful men came to the Berlin home of the young scholar, identified themselves as police officers and took Dr. Gross under their protection to the railroad, from where he was transported to an Austrian insane asylum. Is Dr. Gross mad? It is said that without necessity no father would have his own son locked up as insane. However, in this strange case, the entire circle of friends of the young researcher have raised a public protest and charged that the arrest is the gravest injustice. . . . A large number of scholars, artists, and writers, whose names guarantee they are not motivated by naked sensationalism, have lodged the sharpest protest against the forced internment of Dr. Gross.[6]

The story of the incarceration of Otto Gross, a libertine analyst, by his father, a renowned criminologist, provides the material for a first-rate historical drama; its many acts boast a remarkable cast of characters that include the Grosses themselves, Freud, Jung, Sabina Spielrein, some expressionist writers, and Frieda and D. H. Lawrence. It contains all the elements that Hollywood could dream up: dope addiction, suicides, and love affairs. It also affords a glimpse of the psychoanalytic world when its links to bohemianism, art, and politics still flourished.

Otto Gross and his father were perfectly cast in this drama of generational and cultural collisions. When Otto Gross was spirited away his friends had few doubts that they were witnessing a conflict of cultures; to them, Hans Gross represented an authoritarian and repressive social order challenged by his son and perhaps by psychoanalysis itself. With heavy irony, Franz Jung, an expressionist disciple of Otto Gross, announced that he was supporting Professor Gross, the father: "Hans Gross is old; his life is full of anxiety."[7]

As a criminologist Hans Gross had achieved wide acclaim. As recently as 1962 an edition of his text, *Criminal Investigation*, appeared in English. A preface to this edition notes that the author "acquired by long experience a profound knowledge of the practices of criminals, robbers, tramps, gipsies, cheats. . . ."[8] In life and theory Hans Gross touted the virtues of martial discipline. He established a museum to display the paraphernalia of violence; and he believed that "degenerates," a category that included vagabonds and revolutionaries, should be deported to Africa, since they did not respond to punishment.

Otto Gross personified everything his father fought against and despised: an anarchist, drug addict, psychoanalyst, and exponent of sexual and cultural revolution, he inhabited the bohemian community of Munich. He did everything in excess, including fathering two sons both named Peter born the same year to two women; he also had affairs with both of the von Richthofen sisters, one of whom (Frieda) later became D. H. Lawrence's wife.[9]

Gross deeply impressed everyone he encountered. Freud called him a "gifted, resolute man."[10] He often discussed Gross with Jung, who attempted in a brief analysis to free Gross of dope addiction. "Gross is such a fine man," Freud wrote to Jung, "with such a good mind, that your work must be regarded as a benefit to society."[11] Even Ernest Jones, who met Gross in a cafe, was much taken with him, calling Gross "the nearest approach to the romantic ideal of a genius I have ever met." Never had Jones run across anyone with "such penetrative power of divining the inner thoughts of others."[12]

Impressions of Gross appear in many novels and memoirs of prewar bohemia. In Franz Werfel's novel *The Pure in Heart*, where Gross is represented by the character Gebhart, Gross advances the slogans "Sexual Revolution" and "Abolition of the Family and Middle Class Sex Morality." One character refers to him as "the most remarkable man I ever met—in spite of everything. . . . It's not a question of anything he'd written . . . . It's so hard to define! A wretch, a dope fiend, rather mad, and yet—he was great in himself."[13]

Gross compelled attention by dint of his personality and his

ideas. He preached a doctrine of sexual and cultural emancipation, based on psychoanalytic principles—or his interpretation
of those principles. "The truly healthy state for the neurotic is
sexual immorality. Hence he associates you with Nietzsche."[14]
In these words, Jung, who was treating Gross, summarized for
Freud Gross's ideas. In theory and life Gross championed a
"new ethic" that required "the destruction of monogamy."[15]
Since he believed "authoritarian institutions" crippled humanity, Gross prescribed sexual emancipation as the resolution of
the "cultural crisis." For Gross "the psychology of the unconscious is the philosophy of revolution."[16]

Gross discerned an issue that later troubled radical psychoanalysts, including Wilhelm Reich: authoritarianism in-
fested and distorted the aims of the revolutionaries themselves.
The revolutions of the past failed, Gross declared, because the
revolutionaries harbored an authoritarianism bred by the patriarchal family. They secretly loved the authority they subverted
and reestablished domination when they were able. He proposed that psychoanalysis should help revolutionaries develop
freer sexual relations that would break the chain of patriarchal
authoritarianism. The next revolution will be a revolution not
for father "right" but for mother "right."[17]

Gross deeply touched Jung. As an intellectual font he complicated the already complex relationship between Jung and
Freud. Apart from Jung himself, Freud wrote, only Gross was
capable of "making an original contribution."[18] Indeed Freud
seemed to fear Gross's intellectual creativity or, at least, he
sensed that it was unavoidable that either he himself or Jung
would borrow Gross's ideas. He preferred that Jung treat Gross
so there would no question of "the dividing line between our
respective property rights in creative ideas."[19]

Jung rapidly fell under Gross's spell. "The Gross affair,"
Jung reported to Freud, "has consumed me in the fullest sense
of the word. I have sacrificed days and nights to him." Much

more than a challenging case, Jung saw in Gross's ideas and troubles a reflection of himself. He put it in no uncertain terms: "In Gross I discovered many aspects of my own nature, so that he often seemed like my twin brother."[20]

Although the full extent of Gross's impact on Jung is impossible to measure, Gross's influence was clearly at work in the complicated relations, or "secret symmetry," between Jung and Sabina Spielrein and Spielrein and Freud. At the time of Jung's affair with Spielrein[21]—a young Russian patient of Jung's who later became an analyst and a friend of Freud's—Gross's ideas on freer sexual relations possessed Jung. As Spielrein explained to Freud, she was deeply ambivalent about her feelings for Jung; however, Jung "preached polygamy; his wife was supposed to have no objection, etc. etc."[22] Spielrein described the situation to Freud. She decided to act as the cool patient; but Jung "arrives, beaming with pleasure, and tells me with strong emotion about Gross, about the great insight he has just received (i.e. about polygamy); he no longer wants to suppress his feelings for me."[23] Jung himself obliquely corroborated this to Freud: "During the whole business Gross's notions flittered about a bit too much in my head."[24]

Gross suffered the fate of many psychoanalytic rebels; he was rapidly forgotten by the profession; he died in 1920 at the age of forty-three. His writings were never collected, and he was rarely mentioned. Only a few literary figures and historians kept his memory alive. Franz Jung continued to write on Gross, and when Franz Jung lived in the United States he noted the similarity between the ideas of Gross and Wilhelm Reich, noting as well their similar fates—both were imprisoned.[25] Frieda Lawrence wrote to D. H. Lawrence's biographer, Harry T. Moore, hinting of her affair with Gross many years earlier. "I never told you about my friend, a young Austrian doctor, who had worked with Freud and who revolutionised my life with Freud. Through him and then through me Lawrence knew about Freud."[26]

Gross was more than a curiosity in the history of psychoanalysis. He was hardly representative of the analysts of his day; and Freud did not support his views. Yet by virtue of his ideas, his activities, and his contact with Freud and Jung, Gross exemplified the exuberance and audacity of early psychoanalysis. He belonged to a phase of psychoanalysis which, though it did not endure, left a critical historical legacy. In the development of psychoanalysis, a bohemian moment directly preceded the second generation of political Freudians. They systematized the insights of Gross; and they were sustained by the same classical tradition that engendered Gross.

To move from Gross, who died in 1920, to the second generation of analysts, the political Freudians, who joined the psychoanalytic world in the 1920s, is to enter another terrain. The second generation was no longer composed of isolated rebels or marginal bohemians, but represented sizable groups within psychoanalysis. Politically, intellectually, and socially Fenichel, Reich, Fromm, Bernfeld, and Simmel were not unaccredited outsiders. They could claim many allies; and as teachers and authors they occupied respected psychoanalytic posts.

By the time this second generation emerged, Gross was virtually forgotten. With no psychoanalytic followers, his work disappeared. Theoretically the political Freudians had to begin from scratch. To be sure, Alfred Adler, Paul Federn and a few others injected social categories into psychoanalysis; none left any deep impression on the discipline. Adler rapidly deserted psychoanalysis in favor of common sense; and Federn did not develop his political ideas.[27] Without a compelling body of political psychoanalytic literature, by necessity the political Freudians based themselves squarely on the texts of classical psychoanalysis.

More than any texts, their own experiences served as the raw material for the direction the political Freudians were to take. The youthful experiences of any generation will necessarily prefigure its future conflicts and plans and will determine even its idiom and emotional tone. For the second generation of psychoanalysts—all born within a few years of 1900—there were several decisive influences: the European youth movement, World War I, and the postwar revolutions. These events —they were hardly events, but storms and cyclones—structured their lives. Nearly all the political Freudians participated in the youth movements; as actors or observers, all were affected by the war and subsequent revolutions.

These experiences saturated their youthful lives and ultimately saturated their vision of psychoanalysis. They never viewed psychoanalysis as a medical theory or trade, but as a mission that would bring sense to a disjointed world. Their lives did not possess the coherence and stability that would allow them to think of psychoanalysis as a quiet career choice; rather, they embraced it as a "cause." A major psychoanalytic journal of their generation was called *Psychoanalytische Bewegung* ("The Psychoanalytic Movement") implying an extrascientific almost social dimension. For these Freudians, psychoanalysis was part of a larger project to revamp society. They never surrendered their youthful commitments; as they became analysts they changed only their vocabulary.

World War I had interrupted their lives; and, in retrospect it is clear that Europe never recovered from its violence. Today, after Auschwitz, Hiroshima, and total war, it is difficult to recapture the horror of World War I; we have become inured to the very processes of destruction that it unleashed. "Twentieth-century mass slaughter began in earnest with World War I. About 6,000 people were killed every day for over 1,500 days. The total was around 10 million."[28]

Not only mass death and lethal technologies but also total civilian mobilization marked World War I. Prior to that war, national conflicts seemed distant, discrete, and almost benign. Stefan Zweig in his memoirs, *The World of Yesterday*, asks:

What did the great mass know of war in 1914 after nearly half a century of peace? They did not know war, they had hardly given it a thought. It had become legendary, and distance had made it seem romantic and heroic. They still saw it in the perspective of their school readers and of paintings in museums; brilliant cavalry attacks in glittering uniforms, the fatal shot always straight through the heart, the entire campaign a resounding march of victory—"We'll be home at Christmas," the recruits shouted laughingly to their mothers in August of 1914.[29]

World War I ended this image of war, and ended the nineteenth-century universe of order and calm. Zweig, a biographer and novelist, is a good witness of the cataclysm; he was also its victim. Like many of the analysts, he was born to a wealthy Viennese Jewish family; he recalled the atmosphere before the war as "the Golden Age of Security."

Everything in our almost thousand-year-old Austrian monarchy seemed based on permanency. . . . Everything had its norm, its definite measure and weight . . . everything stood firmly and immovable in its appointed place. . . . No one thought of wars, of revolutions or revolts. All that was radical, all violence, seemed impossible in an age of reason.[30]

World War I shattered like a "hollow vessel of clay" the "world of security and creative reason in which we had been educated, grown up and been at home." For Zweig, for a generation, and for the world, civilization never regained its bearings. Nazism and World War II spread the general insanity and turned Zweig into a transient. Shortly after completing his memoirs in Brazil in 1942, Stefan Zweig, "exhausted by long years of homeless wandering," committed suicide.

The political Freudians were fifteen to twenty years younger than Zweig (1881–1942), and for them the youth movement had already rocked the golden age of security. Indeed the other social earthquakes—the war and postwar revolutions—acted through the youth movement as a single jolt; for the youth movement that the political Freudians knew, lasting roughly from 1915 to 1920, coincided with the period of war and revolution. Fenichel's first writings from within the youth movement date to 1916; his last, those of 1920, breathed of the war's end and the dashed revolutionary hopes. The youth movement mediated these events for its participants. It also served as the one living link to Otto Gross. The same antagonism that infused Gross's life, a revolt of youthful sexuality against a repressive order, animated the youth movement.

Europe and the United States have regularly witnessed youth movements, most recently in the 1960s. The youth movement of the first and seventh decades of the twentieth century resembled each other. Both advanced a slogan of "youth culture"; both rebelled against the style, content, and conformism of bourgeois life; and both placed eros and nature above work and artificiality.

Initially, the German and Austrian youth groups had little to do with politics, but everything to do with a flight from urban civilization. Rooted in the Wandervögel ("roamers" or "ramblers"), a student group at the turn of the century that elevated hiking into a serious activity, the movement spread into an "inchoate revolt against authority."[31] The return to nature resonated in a predominantly Protestant and recently urbanized middle class. The Wandervögel revived folk songs and folk ways, explored the German countryside, and rediscovered or contrived simplicity in dress and behavior. Youths with rucksacks touring backroads became a regular sight. A familiar German nationalism and romanticism almost drowned the implicit protest against industrialization and artifice. The Wandervögel valued the pure and natural relations of an idealized past. Nevertheless, as the Wandervögel broadened into a youth movement, it incorporated many contending factions: educational reformers, utopian socialists, and Zionists, as well as nationalists, anti-Semites, and antifeminists. Its impact extended to the founding of the International Youth Hostel movement in 1907. Youth movements rippled across Europe. Although far more conformist than the German Youth Movement, the same social tensions informed the English boy scout movement.[32]

The left wing of the German movement offered a haven for youths resisting the conventional political choices; instead of choosing among sexual *or* cultural *or* educational reforms, Left circles combined all these aims. Psychoanalysis appeared to be a natural theoretical ally, and youth-movement activists from Siegfried Bernfeld to Rudolf Ekstein regularly graduated into psychoanalysts.[33] After the First World War, Bernfeld, a leader of the Austrian youth movement, argued that psychoanalysis clarified the sexual revolt of youth; to make his point he cited an essay by nineteen-year-old Otto Fenichel on sexual enlightenment.[34]

Youths who studied or dabbled in psychoanalysis formed a fraction of an increasingly factionalized movement. Indeed, as the various splits deepened, youth leaders attempted to unify the movement. The convention they called for October 1913 to resolve differences marked a crucial event in the history of the youth movement. Its date, the centennial of the Battle of Leipzig or the German victory over Napoleon, signified the nationalist impulse of the movement; its location, a mountaintop, signified its cult of nature as well as its distance from the official celebration on the actual battle site.

The groups and individuals who converged on Meissner Mountain represented a wide political spectrum.[35] While no unity resulted, a new and more political grouping, the Free German Youth, emerged. This group proposed a principle, known as the Meissner formula, to unify the youth movement. The formula was sufficiently vague as to be interpreted to the satisfaction of almost everyone. Fenichel frequently returned to it: "Free German Youth, on their own initiative, under their own responsibility, and with deep sincerity, are determined to independently shape their own lives."[36]

Fenichel's writings and activities during this period lie within a triangle delineated by three participants in the Meissner Mountain convention: Gustav Wyneken, Siegfried Bernfeld, and Alfred Kurella. In a political spectrum ranging from right to left, Wyneken, Bernfeld, and Kurella represented, respectively, degrees of educational reform, social transformation, and sexual liberation. All of their lives were intertwined. For instance, Bernfeld edited a journal inspired by Wyneken; Fenichel published in one of Wyneken's journals as well as in Bernfeld's own journal; and Kurella championed Wyneken just as Fenichel championed Kurella.

To psychoanalysts, only Bernfeld's name might spark recognition, perhaps for his studies of Freud, which Ernest Jones has praised.[37] During the World War I period, when Fenichel was closely linked with him, Bernfeld energetically promoted Zionism, socialism, and psychoanalysis. A talented organizer and powerful speaker, he continually established new political groups, called conferences, and founded institutions which often did not endure. Like many youth-movement leaders he considered school reform as fundamental; and he set up alternatives to schools, where youths might gather free from sexual and class domination.[38] Freud once commended him as "perhaps the strongest head among my students and followers. In addition, he is of superior knowledge, an overwhelming speaker and an extremely powerful teacher."[39]

The lives of Bernfeld and Fenichel ran in parallel paths. Both were born to Jewish Viennese families; both attended the University of Vienna; both participated in left-wing youth movements, although Bernfeld—five years older—acted more as a leader and organizer; both were intellectually precocious and delivered psychoanalytic papers as very young men. They both remained loyal to their original political radicalism and were active in left-wing psychoanalytic circles. Both moved to Berlin, emigrated to the United States, and died in California. Significantly, neither is remembered as a political theorist.

Bernfeld praised Fenichel's "Sexual Enlightenment," which was published in a series on the youth movement edited by Max Hodann who, years later, sympathetically examined Reich's "Sex-Pol," his effort to spread sexual knowledge to the working class.[40] "Sexual Enlightenment" drew upon a questionnaire of sexual experiences that Fenichel conducted while still a Gymnasium student; the essay provisionally interpreted the fifty-four replies he received.[41] In a prefatory note to the article, Hodann requested that for the sake of science additional replies be sent to Fenichel; they should include such information as sex of respondent, age at time of "sexual enlightenment," its circumstances and consequences. The statistical approach remained a favorite of Fenichel's. Fifteen years after conducting this survey he wrote a statistical account of the therapeutic results of the Berlin Psychoanalytic Institute.[42]

While "Sexual Enlightenment" already rallied to psychoanalysis, Fenichel realized that enlisting psychoanalysis on behalf of sexual reforms required care. Referring to Freud, Fenichel observes that the "external factors" of sexual enlightenment are often overemphasized, and the "inner factors"

neglected. Youths generally hear and understand sexual information when they are psychically prepared. Such information
necessarily arouses anxiety. Prior to puberty sexual information
is repressed, ignored, or forgotten, but, with the onset of puberty, individuals are ready for sexual enlightenment.[43]

This developmental schema might trouble a sexual reformer,
since it suggests that exterior reforms are irrelevant to the
sexual life of the individual. Fenichel was at pains to qualify
this implication. Although the impact of social experience is
sometimes exaggerated, he claimed, it is hardly insignificant.
Sexual education is currently disastrous; nor is the damage
corrected by parents who are silent about sexuality so not to
disturb their children. Stress cannot be completely avoided.
However "all our conflicts spring from sexuality; and if we are
able to affirm sexuality, rendering it clear and simple," gratui-
tous pain will be eliminated.[44]

To illustrate the danger of imperfect sexual knowledge, Fenichel referred to Frank Wedekind's *Spring's Awakening*. A
favorite of Fenichel's, he rarely wrote an essay in these years
without mentioning it. In 1920, Fenichel published an appreciation of the play in *Der Neue Anfang* ("The New Beginning"),
a journal linked to Bernfeld and Wyneken. Many youth reformers shared Fenichel's enthusiasm for the play, a probing
of adolescent sexuality mangled by adult authoritarianism and
callousness. Censored as pornographic for fifteen years, it was
first staged in 1906, and constantly performed over the next
several years.[45] While Wedekind caricatured the teachers
(Professors Breakneck, Tonguetwister, Total Loss), he presented the parents as well meaning but crippled by convention-
ality. Fenichel often alluded to the scene where Wendla, at
fourteen, beseeches her mother to give her sexual information.
"Don't get cross, Mamma, don't get cross. There's no one I
can ask but you. Please, dear Mamma, please do tell me

. . . . D'you think it's any easier for me?" Mamma tries but is unable to eke out more than the standard fairy tales.[46]

The play is littered with youthful victims. Moritz, tormented by sexual desire and ignorance, kills himself after his humiliating failure of a Gymnasium examination. "If I fail my father would have a stroke, and my mother a breakdown," he had warned. Melchior, his best friend, is expelled for giving accurate sexual information to Moritz. Wendla dies at the hands of an abortionist. Fenichel defended the play as subtle and accurate, roundly rejecting charges that it exaggerated Gymnasium life. Only adults distant from students and school can deny the truths of *Spring's Awakening*. According to Fenichel, Wedekind was an intuitive genius of psychological life.

Fenichel mentioned in passing that he himself was threatened by expulsion from the Gymnasium for collecting the statistics on sexual enlightenment. His identification with Melchior, who was expelled for transmitting sexual knowledge, probably goes further. Melchior was the best student at the Gymnasium as well as the most resilient. Allusions to a lecture he delivers to Moritz ("You think you're safe, sailing untouched past the Scylla of all that religious nonsense, and there's the Charybdis of omens and superstitions waiting to suck you down") regularly reappeared in Fenichel's youthful essays. Finally, Melchior is the only partial victor in the play, punished but not defeated.

At the same time as this appreciation, Fenichel completed a book, which was never published, on the sexual question in the youth movement.[47] Only the last chapter, summarizing his observations, survives. He outlines typical sexual conflicts of youth and notes that nearly everywhere the youth movement made steady progress against simple repression. Nevertheless despite improvement Fenichel observes that both politics and religion complicated the sexual question. In 1920 he reviewed at length a book on sexual ethics directed at young Jews. The book set forth a Draconian sexual code of purity, asceticism, and chastity in the name of a Jewish tradition.

Fenichel, identifying himself as a "sexologist and conscious young Jew," vigorously denounced the book. His stridency prompted the editor to append a note stating that the journal was deviating from usual reviewing practices—not to commission reviews from parties involved in the book—since it seemed worthwhile that a participant in the Jewish youth movement review the work.[48] "In the name of our female friends, in the name of Judaism, in the name of mind *(Geist)*," writes Fenichel, "we protest out of our deepest soul against the identification of prostitution and premarital sexuality." The asceticism advanced here would bring about crippling neurosis and would even damage the cultural activities the author wants to encourage.

We are Jewish youth. And we would be neither Jewish nor youth if we submitted to any authority simply because it was authority. . . . For us, no tradition is holy! We do not wish to be what our fathers were, but we wish to be what has never been. 'Jewish' for us is not the ghetto morality, and not even the ethics of biblical Israel; Jewish is the core of our souls. . . . Jewish is not the past but the future![49]

Fenichel concluded by affirming that the few words in Siegfried Bernfeld's *Jüdisches Volk und seine Jugend* ("Jewish People and Its Youth") on sexual ethics were incomparably "more profound, more Jewish and more youthful" than the entire book under review.

The question of Jews haunted the German and Austrian youth movements;[50] the affection for a pure nature and a simple past often tilted toward a virulent German nationalism and anti-Semitism. A renewal of anti-Semitism after the Meissner Mountain conference prompted Bernfeld to attempt to unify Jewish youth in Vienna.[51] Enlisting the aid of Martin

Buber, Bernfeld set up an Austrian Jewish Youth Conference in 1918.[52] He also founded a new journal, *Jerubbaal*, and an accompanying organization of Jewish youth, the "Order Jerubbaal."

According to the psychoanalyst Willi Hoffer, who helped Bernfeld in running an innovative home for Jewish orphans, *Jerubbaal* was more than a "literary mouthpiece"; it was a "battle cry" of youth dedicated to a cause.[53] Bernfeld explained in an introduction to the journal that it would encourage Jewish youth to recognize their own value in opposition to an adult and non-Jewish world. Adults only wanted to educate Jewish youth into mature members of the bourgeoisie; the non-Jews sought to persecute and insult Jews.[54] The life of the journal was brief, lasting only a year. It is not clear if Fenichel belonged to the Order Jerubbaal; however, he was a member of a successor group,[55] and he did contribute to the journal.

Pulsating with expressionism, Nietzsche, and political upheaval, Fenichel's contribution to *Jerubbaal*, "Esoterik" (1919), smacked of post–World War I Germany. Fenichel did not define the esoteric as mystical, which, following Nietzsche, he considered superficial. The esoteric was secret, but its secrecy was not intrinsic. Those unafraid of discomfort and philosophical rigor, the truly honest and serious, could enter its realm; it was off limits to the philistines and to the timid. The "last" secret lesson taught that "one must be honest," a verity "the truly initiated" will understand.

Fenichel sought to transcend a simple rationalism and materialism not by irrationalism but by a richer rationalism. "Esoterik" was partly directed against a conventional and academic socialism. A politics that remains on the surface cannot reach the deeper driving forces of will and desire. For Fenichel, a deadening routinization endangered ordinary politics and politicians. When a dire world situation makes us forget ourselves, we become our worst enemies: "politicians."

In the essay, Fenichel affirms that "politics exists for humanity and not humanity for politics." He cites from the Meissner Mountain formula of self-determination in accord with inner truth. The usual objection that before cultural demands may be met, people must "eat" is accurate, he states; but it is also an excuse and flight from cultural commitment. We must also know what we want; to escape from the meaninglessness of life we need a direction. Rationalism provides a means, not an end, and cheap party programs are of no help. "Self-observation, self-value and self-change" are required. "No more self-deception." "For us nothing is holy any longer. No dogma—nothing —is beyond criticism. . . . Only what understanding can justify deserves to exist."[56]

The Nietzschean and expressionist tones of "Esoterik" suggest the two other coordinates of the Meissner Mountain triangle of Fenichel's thought: Alfred Kurella and Gustav Wyneken. It was only at the least typical phases of their lives, when they were inching toward a political expressionism, that their paths crossed with Fenichel's. Today only experts on Communist officialdom would be able easily to identify Kurella. In his later years, he became a Soviet citizen and a top functionary of East Germany—a very long way from his days in the youth movement.[57] During the period of the First World War he championed a program of sexual freedom, expressionism, and extreme leftism. He was far from a conventional Marxist and attracted attention more for his guide on playing the lute and his ideas on free love than for a doctrine of class struggle. He participated in the extreme Left of the youth movement, but finally Kurella's more standard political identification proved decisive. In 1919 he traveled to Moscow, met Lenin, and, upon his return, joined the German Communist party.[58]

Unlike Kurella, who was important only to a sexual and political Left, Wyneken exercised a great influence on the youth movement as a whole.[59] He was an educational reformer who cofounded a Free School at Wickersdorf. Against the tenor of German education, democratic and humanitarian values permeated his school. However, Wyneken was more than a local educational reformer. He was a forceful speaker and propagandist. Wyneken, who espoused "youth culture," believed that once youth discovered its own value, it would offer a viable alternative to an adult and philistine world. In Wyneken the left wing of the youth movement found a program and vocabulary, although he himself was not a socialist.

With revolution in the air at the war's end, the programs of educational reform, sexual freedom, and cultural emancipation lost their sharp edges and merged into overlapping projects. When the school administrators turned against Wyneken and discharged him, Kurella came to his defense.[60] At the same time that Kurella was drifting toward the expressionist left, events pushed Wyneken in that direction. Both were associated with *Der Aufbruch*, which briefly flickered as an expressionist antiwar journal; it included the writings of the anarchist Gustav Landauer, who was later murdered in the revolution in Bavaria.[61]

Conventional categories of spirit and politics, love and struggle, fail to do justice to the ideas of Kurella and his collaborators. They sought to propel the youth movement in a socialist, and then Communist direction, believing that youth itself constituted a "counter" bourgeois class.[62] Yet the political vocabulary did not suffocate their youth-movement idiom. If Kurella urged that youth side with the proletariat,[63] the goal was not socialism but "community."[64] The group Kurella joined, "Decisive Youth," did not call for a proletarian state, but a party of youth.[65] Politics and culture joined hands. The issues that later animated Marxists such as Lukács and Karl Korsch had already been enunciated by these cultural radicals: monochromatic political change does not constitute a revolution if human and cultural relations remain unchanged; nor can human transformation be adjourned until the victory of the socialist revolution.

For Kurella and his colleagues, revolution required the convergence of political and social change. Kurella called for a "new man" and culture to accompany and, perhaps, precede the political restructuring.[66] These ideas percolated throughout Kurella's group, Decisive Youth, which later entered the Communist party. "The cultural components of the communist society must not and cannot wait until the political-economic victory of communism," stated the program of Decisive Youth. The bourgeoisie announces its future political victories through cultural advances; the Communists must follow suit.[67]

The components of freedom that could not be delayed included sexual reform. On this issue, Fenichel drew close to Kurella. Beyond a general leftism, Kurella made his name by promoting a brand of sexual mysticism or *Körperseele* ("body-soul"). In Berlin and Vienna followers of Kurella preached free love and sexual emancipation.[68] In a number of youth and expressionist journals, Kurella spelled out his almost spiritual doctrine.[69] Denouncing the sexual asceticism that was promoted by some sections of the youth movement, he maintained that natural instincts must be allowed expression. However, free expression did not signal sexual promiscuity. Sexual contact parallels and depends on spiritual contact; the meeting of the bodies was unthinkable without the meeting of the souls. Although Kurella militantly championed sexual emancipation, and specifically defended premarital sexuality, the mystical dimensions of his doctrine threatened to drown the simpler issues of sexual freedom.

Fenichel lauded Kurella's ideas and participated in his circle. Praising him in a pamphlet Kurella edited, Fenichel baldly states that the doctrine of "body-soul" marked a "turning point in the history of the youth movement." Prior to Kurella the youth movement had dismissed the phrases "self-determination" and "inner truth" (from the Meissner formula); with few exceptions inanities filled literature on sexuality. Kurella is challenging us to become what we are. Fenichel quotes him: "Only when we dare to express and fulfill what is; when we take responsibility for our entire being . . . then we take the first step to a new land."

Fenichel, in the pamphlet, translates the Meissner formula into a sexual idiom; inner truth, self-determination, and self-understanding gained a subversive sexual meaning. A serious examination of the Meissner formula, states Fenichel, requires a "transformation of sexuality." Kurella has begun to show the way; now it is necessary to take the next step, bringing theory and fact into accord. "Affirmation of oneself means affirmation of one's sexuality." There are no transcendental ethical systems; sexuality is relative, complex, and unique. As long as society is not damaged, any sexual behavior, including non-monogamous relations, is acceptable. It is not sexuality but rather asceticism that is destructive: "Only the transformation of sexuality can remedy our contemporary and crippled situation."[70]

A final text with the modest title "Reflections on Luserke's Book" closed the period that "Esoterik" had recently opened; it was Fenichel's farewell to his youthful activities and hopes, his last piece that still breathed of a sexual-social revolution. Martin Luserke, an educational reformer, succeeded Wyneken at Wickersdorf.[71] His book, which inspired Fenichel, was drenched with the German revolution, already past. "We do not want any reforms; we want revolutions in the schools."[72] However, Fenichel hardly mentions the book; in the spirit of "Esoterik," his review is a Nietzschean mediation on the events in Germany. In the nine months since "Esoterik," Fenichel concludes, our hopes have been dashed. We have endured war, but not this great disappointment. What happened,

he asks, to the time in November 1918 when we youths believed in Gustav Landauer, revolution, and Geist? It has all
ended with murder, trials, and Noske.[73]

Like "Esoterik," "Reflections" expresses a dissatisfaction
with conventional politics, including radical politics. Fenichel
in these essays does not write off politics, rather, simple political transformation is not sufficient. Revolutionaries must
change themselves as well as the social conditions; both the
cultural and subjective dimensions must be renovated. An accompanying article on Luserke's book by Eckart Peterich presents the same argument. When the German revolution
began, we "the followers of Wyneken and the youth cultural
movement joined its ranks," but our efforts came to nothing.
"We turned to the revolutionary parties and tried to influence
their school platforms" and went from defeat to defeat. Like
Fenichel, Peterich did not break with socialism or revolution.
In Luserke he found a renewal of the authentic socialism of
Landauer and Marx.[74]

Fenichel paints a grim picture of contemporary Germany in
"Reflections"; despair, chaos, and gallows humor crowd the
streets. After the numbing expenditure of energy, collapse and
fatigue have set in. However, he warns we should not let any
cries of "Long Live the Revolution!" divert us from finding the
truth. Fenichel does not attribute defeat solely to the authorities and police; rather the defeats inhered in the individuals.
The causes are interior as well as exterior: "Even more than
Noske, everyone is defeated by themselves." Fenichel calls not
for the end of politics, but for the end of conventional politics.
He wants a renewal of education and utopia, the efforts to
change the stuff of humanity itself. A superficial politics that
circumvents the human material may obtain rapid results but
cannot endure. "The Bolsheviks are not radical; but Luserke's
book is. . . . The new education creates the new humanity and
this creates the new world."[75]

One passage in "Reflections" succinctly presents Fenichel's position; and although it does not cite Marx, it seems to be directly responding to his principles. It also succeeds in summarizing the experiences and lessons of the youth movement. The young Marx had written: "To be radical is to grasp things by the root. But for man the root is man himself." Marx goes on to say that the critique of religion concludes with the imperative to subvert the conditions that debase man.[76] Months after the defeat of the German revolution, and seventy-five years after Marx's statement, Fenichel altered its emphasis. Marx was leaving behind the Utopian educators; Fenichel was returning to them:

No revolution changes the essentials so long as it only changes the institutions and ignores the men who live by them. If humanity is a function of institutions, so are institutions a function of humanity. For a transformation of the world to be radical it must grasp things by the root. The root is man. Education changes man. This is the path that is given to us.[77]

# CHAPTER THREE

# The Berlin Institute:
# The Politics of
# Psychoanalysis

WHEN Fenichel moved to Berlin from Vienna in 1922 to complete his psychoanalytic training, he entered a world of acrimonious politics and explosive social conflicts. Violence plagued the new German Republic from its commencement in World War I to its destruction in arson with the burning of the Reichstag, the German parliament. The fifteen years of Weimar Germany (1918–33) were disrupted by continuous political assassinations and putsches, which frightened liberal forces, and economic crises, which devastated the working and middle classes. In 1922 one dollar bought 4,500 marks; in 1923 one dollar fetched 4.2 trillion marks. The economy recovered, although the German people did not. Within seven years another economic explosion, the world Depression of 1929, traumatized the gun-shy population.

# The Berlin Institute: The Politics of Psychoanalysis

These were not years of quiet and peaceful retreat. As the economy worsened in the early 1930s and the Nazis flourished, even those usually indifferent to politics were sucked into the fray. The stakes were high, immediate, and obvious: the preservation of democracy or the creation of a new Nazi Reich. Neutrality was barely possible. Young political psychoanalysts who had already been baptized by the youth movement, World War I, and the postwar revolutions needed little prompting. They had turned to psychoanalysis to reform the world. As Weimar Germany stumbled toward nazism, collapse, or revolution, the younger analysts—Fenichel, Reich, Bernfeld, Fromm, and dozens of others—assembled to evaluate the political relevance of their discipline.

They gathered in Berlin. In the 1920s Berlin's crackling atmosphere of politics and culture attracted the political psychoanalysts. Moreover the geographic insulation from Freud allowed theoretical and political heresies almost impossible under his nose. As a Berlin analytic couple put it, in Vienna Freud's students were "all oppressed" by "the Giant." On the other hand, rebellious analysts found in Berlin "a feeling of freedom."[1] Many of the Berlin analysts did in fact become theoretical rebels—among them, Karen Horney, Franz Alexander, and Melanie Klein—while the Viennese remained theoretically (and politically) more conservative—for example, Heinz Hartmann, Robert Waelder, and Ernst Kris. Wilhelm Reich, who moved from Vienna to Berlin, concluded that the Berlin analysts were "far more progressive in social matters than the Viennese."[2]

The Berlin Institute, founded by Freud's followers in 1920, predated a formal institute in Vienna.[3] Students from around the world applied to the Berlin Institute, which also boasted a superb teaching staff from Karl Abraham to Otto Fenichel and Melanie Klein.[4] As a center of psychoanalytic training and education Vienna never could compete with Berlin. Only after the rise of Hitler did the hub of psychoanalytic activity briefly revert to Vienna.[5]

The Berlin Institute itself reflected a social and political openness. From its origin it was infused by a civic spirit, even a mission. Initially it devoted its resources to providing therapy to those lacking the private means. As Freud stated at its tenth anniversary, the Berlin Institute endeavored "to make our therapy accessible to the great numbers of people who suffer no less than the rich from neurosis, but are not in a position to pay for treatment."[6]

Freud's remarks were more than a ritual expression of public beneficence. Social principles motivated Max Eitingon and Ernst Simmel, the founders of the Berlin Institute; they wanted to emancipate psychoanalysis from an exclusive reliance on wealthy neurotics. Simmel himself was a socialist, and his activities, again, demonstrate the close links between socialism and classical psychoanalysis.

Although fifteen years older than Fenichel, Simmel's life roughly paralleled his younger associate's.[7] From the founding of the Berlin Institute and the founding of Schloss Tegel, the first psychoanalytic sanatarium, to presiding over the Society of Socialist Physicians, a socialist impulse permeated Simmel's activities.[8] Like Fenichel, he died in California, and like the other political Freudians he maintained a low political profile in the United States. At the end of his life, Simmel organized a conference on anti-Semitism, "a social disease." Perhaps the last hurrah of the political Freudians, it brought together Simmel, Fenichel, and Bernfeld of the political Freudians and Max Horkheimer and T. W. Adorno of the neo-Marxist Frankfurt School.[9]

Freud highly esteemed Simmel, conferring on him honorary membership in his original committee. "I don't know of anyone in Berlin who, by the purity and intensity of his allegiance would be more worthy of inclusion in that circle—if it still existed."[10] From one of Freud's frequent visits to Simmel's sanatarium, located outside of Berlin, comes a lovely story of Freud the mordant social critic. Simmel recounts:

> Once while walking about the grounds of the Sanitarium we came to a place where a large police dog was chained. I knew him to be vicious and he was released only at night to watch the premises. I warned Freud not to go near him.
>
> "Please keep away from him Professor. He's very vicious."
>
> Freud gave me a gently admonishing smile, calmly stepped up to the dog and released him. And while the huge dog gratefully lept upon the fragile form of the Professor, who patted his newest follower, Freud said to me:
>
> "If you had been chained up all your life, you'd be vicious too."[11]

A 1918 lecture by Freud, possibly his sharpest reminder of the social obligation of psychoanalysis, directly inspired Simmel and Eitingon to set up the Berlin Institute. Freud asserted that "the large masses of people" suffer from neurosis as much as the smaller numbers of rich. "The necessities of our own existence limit our work to the well-to-do classes." However "the poor man has just as much right to help for his mind." For this reason Freud dreamed a "fantastic" idea which "belongs to the future" when "the conscience of the community will awake" and provide free psychoanalytic care.[12]

That Freud delivered this lecture in Budapest in 1918 may not have been completely accidental. Hungary—all of Europe —rumbled with revolution. Within weeks of Freud's lecture a republic was established in Budapest; within several months Lenin sent his greetings to its successor government, the Hungarian Soviet Republic. Lenin may not have been aware that the Hungarian Soviet Republic appointed Ferenczi to a post at the University of Budapest, the first academic position in psychoanalysis;[13] however, his appointment lasted no longer than the government itself—some one hundred days.

With Freud's fantastic dream as a spur, Simmel and Eitingon set up the Berlin Institute to provide psychoanalytic therapy to the less-than-rich.[14] Later, in language never again used by establishment psychoanalysis, Eitingon bemoaned the decline of "authentic proletarian elements" and the rise of bourgeois intellectuals among Institute patients.[15] Ernest Jones observes how the Institute originally served the poor, but gradually shifted its focus to psychoanalytic education.[16]

Although the Berlin Institute embraced liberal and social values, for the younger analysts its formality and hierarchical structure discouraged open political discussions. For this reason, Fenichel, who was on the official teaching staff, organized and led a seminar outside the Institute. This was the so-called Children's Seminar, a locus of activity for younger dissident analysts.[17] It was an unofficial left-leaning seminar infused—to use Fenichel's words—with the spirit of "democratic camaraderie."[18] It lasted the life of the Institute or, more exactly, until most of the analysts fled before nazism.

Accounts of the Seminar's origin differ. According to Simmel, Fenichel offered a seminar which some older analysts attacked for overemphasizing the nexus between psychoanalysis and socialism. Fenichel spurned the criticism and triggered a rebellion of younger teachers and candidates. "His reaction was 'What of it? If you don't like the way we do it—let us be naughty children.' From then on this seminar became famous under the official title 'The Children's Seminar.' "[19] In Fenichel's account, however, he did not lead a rebellion of socialist psychoanalysts against the authorities. Rather Eitingon suggested that the younger candidates might profit from discussions conducted outside the official curriculum. Fenichel adopted the suggestion, and in November 1924 the first meeting of the Children's Seminar took place.[20]

# The Berlin Institute: The Politics of Psychoanalysis

Fenichel (along with Harold Schultz-Hencke) dominated the Children's Seminar.[21] The group met every few weeks at the private homes of participants. According to Fenichel's careful accounting, there were 168 meetings at which the number of participants varied from five to twenty. The title of Fenichel's lecture, given in October of 1933 at the last meeting before they all dispersed speaks for itself: "Psychoanalysis, Socialism and the Tasks for the Future." All of Fenichel's closest associates participated in the Children's Seminar: the Reichs, the Bornsteins, Francis Deri, Edith Jacobson, Barbara Lantos, Kate Friedländer, and Erich Fromm, among others.

Yet the Children's Seminar did not espouse a specific politics; at least, the titles of the papers and themes of discussions do not reveal a sharp political orientation. The informality and internal disagreements within the seminar prompted the formation of a smaller and tighter political grouping. According to Edith Jacobson, a left-wing group split off from the Children's Seminar and met privately. It included among its members Jacobson herself, Fenichel, the Reichs, Fromm, and Gero. "We specifically dealt with therapeutic 'character' problems, discussed Reich's ideas, and also socio-psychological questions."[22]

The political realities increasingly rendered the discussions of the left-wing psychoanalysts more than an amusing intellectual pastime. Few were untouched by the economic collapse of 1929 and the looming threat of nazism. "Berlin was in a state of civil war," wrote Isherwood in *The Berlin Stories*. The economic depression ravaged Germany and fueled the Nazis; more than half the labor force was unemployed. In 1930, the Nazis became the second largest party, capturing six and a half million votes.

The crisis propelled many intellectuals leftward. "The city was in a state of fever," recalled Gustav Regler in his great memoir *The Owl of Minerva*.

We lived in a block of flats which had been built with the aid of a state subsidy and was reserved for the use of artists and writers. It was cheap, but scarcely one of the occupants was able to pay his rent . . . . People ate their meals off packing-cases covered with newspaper . . . . To live surrounded by universal poverty and hardship was to become readily receptive to a revolutionary creed. There is no need for involved, ideological explanation for my reasons for joining the Communist Party. It can be summed up in a sentence—"Things can't go on like this!"[23]

Things did go on like that; and in this atmosphere Reich, Fromm, Fenichel, Bernfeld, and others gathered to weigh the political import of psychoanalysis. Since the earlier efforts of Gross or Federn, the cultural situation had changed. Analytic groups devoted to a political psychoanalysis now regularly formed. The opening salvo of the renewed attention to a political psychoanalysis belonged to Bernfeld; his *Sisyphus or the Limits of Education* (1925) expressed the sentiments of many analysts bucking the orthodoxies: "Both Marx and Freud are right, though not the Marxists or the Freudians."[24]

Within the small analytic world of Berlin, the political Freudians composed a close community. The analysts gathered for a 1926 lecture by Bernfeld testified to the tight web of relations. He delivered an address, "Socialism and Psychoanalysis," to the Society of Socialist Physicians. At the lecture Ernst Simmel and Barbara Lantos offered comments. Bernfeld, Simmel, and Lantos were all involved with Fenichel. Bernfeld's relationship with him reached back a number of years; Lantos joined Fenichel's inner circle and received the *Rundbriefe;* and Simmel was a friend who ultimately enabled Fenichel to emigrate to the United States. Fenichel himself reviewed Bernfeld's lecture when it was published, commending Bernfeld for grasping the issues "incomparably deeper and more precisely than his predecessors."[25]

# The Berlin Institute: The Politics of Psychoanalysis

By 1930 all of Fenichel's group had assembled in Berlin and were participating in the activities of the political Freudians. Edith Jacobson had finished her medical training in Munich and had come to Berlin for her analytic training.[26] Annie Reich, who shared a past with Fenichel in the Austrian youth movement, had arrived in Berlin with her husband Wilhelm Reich.[27] Kate Friedländer had received her medical degree and entered the Berlin Institute in 1926.[28] George Gero, who was Hungarian, had begun his analytic training in Berlin in 1924; he interrupted it to obtain a philosophy degree, and then returned to the Berlin Institute in 1930.[29] The other Hungarians, Barbara Lantos[30] and Edith Ludowyk Gyömröi,[31] had also arrived in Berlin after stops in Vienna.

The political Freudians were soon faced with the disintegrating situation of Germany and some hard choices. Not only had the Nazi threat intensified, but the Social Democrats and the Communists had succumbed to fratricide. The Communists directed their "main blow" and main fury against the Social Democrats. The period of a broad anti-Fascist coalition—the popular front—belonged to the future. In this tense situation the politicized psychoanalysts were forced to choose between the Social Democrats and the Communists.

Many Berlin analysts, such as Simmel and Bernfeld, drew close to the Social Democrats.[32] The circles of Reich and Fenichel moved toward the Communist party. Reich became a party member. Barbara Lantos may have joined also; she married a Communist who had fled to the Soviet Union after the collapse of the Hungarian Soviet Republic. The Berlin Institute had initially rejected Edith L. Gyömröi as "too red." She also became a Communist party member. Like Wilhelm Reich, Gyömröi was expelled from the party during the first years of exile.[33] It is not clear whether Edith Jacobson and Kate Friedländer enlisted.

If Fenichel evolved from a radical youth and socialist into a Communist, it would not have been surprising; yet it is not certain whether he ever joined the Communist party. His last work still hinting of the youth movement, "Psychoanalysis and Metaphysics" (1923), called for a "new ethics,"[34] while his first work devoted to psychoanalysis and socialism dated from 1928. If Fenichel did not join the Communist party in the ensuing years, he was very sympathetic to its politics and to the Soviet Union. He could be labeled a "fellow traveler."

Like many devotees of the Soviet Union, he visited the home of revolution several times. After one visit he published a brief article describing his tour of a prison for youthful offenders, Bolschevo, outside of Moscow. While he qualified that a single visit does not allow a searching investigation, he enthusiastically praised what he had seen. Bolschevo fundamentally differed from similar institutions in capitalist countries. It was "unmistakable" how "pleasing" was the organization of life. Individuals conducted themselves with "devotion" and "pride." An atmosphere of "freedom and good will permeated the place."[35]

Fenichel's enthusiasm for Bolschevo placed him in distinguished company. A veritable army of Western fellow travelers traipsed through Bolschevo, a showcase prison which the Soviets put on many itineraries. André Gide, Sidney and Beatrice Webb, Harold Laski, and many others returned with glowing reports of communism in action at Bolschevo. Gide states that "nothing could be more edifying, more reassuring and encouraging than this visit."[36] The Webbs in their *Soviet Communism: A New Civilization* conclude that Bolschevo was closer to an "ideal treatment of offenders against society than anything else in the world."[37] Yet Bolschevo was an exhibition for Western visitors;[38] few had the resources and, perhaps, the inclination to challenge its authenticity. David Caute in his study *The Fellow-Travellers* notes that "the majority of visitors were led straight to Bolschevo with its model factories, libraries and educational factories. . . . It was only after his return to France that Gide discovered that Bolschevo was packed with privileged informers."[39]

By the early 1930s the issues of a Marxist psychoanalysis occupied Fenichel. He lectured frequently on the social implications of psychoanalysis to a number of left-wing analytic groups, the Psychoanalytic Marxist Group, the Analytic Marxist Group, and the Marxist-Analytic Workshop. The subject of Fenichel's last lecture in Berlin before exile was psychoanalysis and socialism; the title of his first in Oslo was "Psychoanalysis and Marxism."

The writings he published in this period reflecting these concerns are not voluminous; they include an evaluation of a special issue devoted to politics of a psychoanalytic journal, an article on Erich Fromm, and several reviews of Wilhelm Reich. The first article, on the psychoanalysis of politics, blasts René Laforgue for confounding psychoanalytic and political truths. Fenichel accuses Laforgue of failing to distinguish between the individual and society. He justified social misery and authoritarianism in the name of the sadomasochism of the masses.[40] A conventional Marxism informs the much longer unpublished manuscript of Fenichel's critique of Laforgue; Fenichel defends the Soviet Union from an assortment of charges by echoing the almost official position: while the Soviet Union had not yet established a classless society, it was moving in that direction.

Fenichel reviewed with warmth the works of Fromm and Reich. He lauded Fromm's programmatic essay, subtitled "Notes on Psychoanalysis and Historical Materialism," which appeared in the Frankfurt School journal.[41] Signaling its "happy agreement" with Reich, Fenichel judged it of "fundamental importance" for a social psychoanalysis.

71

If someone objects that it is not possible for sociologically "neutral" psychoanalysts to embrace one-sidedly the "still debatable" historical materialism, then the counterquestion must be posed: how is social psychoanalytic work possible without a social position?[42]

Fenichel regularly reviewed Reich's work, often tempering his praise with criticism. He judged *Der treibhafte Charakter* ("The Impulsive Character"), published in 1925, an extremely thoughtful book. "Unfortunately it is very weakened in many places by a formal and terminological inexactness."[43] In the early 1930s Fenichel praised a series of works that left no doubt about his essential agreement with Reich. Reich, he stated, possessed the "courage" to set forth in a popular pamphlet the connection between sexual morality and the capitalist system.[44] He described another of Reich's works as "the first effort to bring psychoanalytic knowledge to bear on a Marxist critique of the social-sexual order."[45]

In a lengthy review of Reich's *The Function of the Orgasm*, however, Fenichel went beyond simple endorsement to suggest the differences that were later to divide them. He considered the clinical description first rate but the theory was "unfortunately not always clear." For Fenichel, Reich offered an incomplete account of anxiety; he abandoned "too soon" a psychological approach for a somatic and biological explanation.

Nor did Fenichel find acceptable Reich's pronouncement that the proletariat suffered less sexual repression than the ruling class. That the sadism of the ruling class was founded on its own sexual repression and that this repression facilitated the subjugation of the proletariat were not serious sociological ideas, concluded Fenichel. He questioned

whether Reich again exaggerates when he views satisfying sexual intercourse as a causa sine qua non of psychic health. . . . There are people who are without any particular neurotic disturbances, and live sexually unsatisfied; indeed, it seems to us, that the ability to endure without disturbance some dissatisfaction, should be seen as belonging exactly to the criterion of full health.[46]

This review broached problems that eventually pulled Fenichel and Reich apart; it stands as proof that theoretical differences predated their political squabbling in exile. Fenichel believed Reich risked theoretical simplification, biologism, and a fetish of genital sexuality. Yet these issues were not yet divisive; during this same period, Fenichel reviewed Reich's "Dialectic Materialism and Psychoanalysis" and commended it to readers "who might not be able to go as far with Reich as can the reviewer." Additional efforts by Reich, Fenichel suggested, would be especially welcomed by psychoanalysts who are also socialists.[47]

Reich's "Dialectical Materialism and Psychoanalysis" had appeared in an official Communist publication, *Unter dem Banner des Marxismus* ("Under the Banner of Marxism"); its editors noted that they did not share Reich's appreciation of psychoanalysis.[48] The Soviet receptivity to psychoanalysis was brief, and by 1930 long past.[49] Barely tolerated by the Soviets, Reich was eventually expelled from the Communist party.

How the Soviet hostility to psychoanalysis affected Fenichel's politics is a matter of conjecture. After 1932, his statements on the Soviet Union became uniformly vague; there is no reason to believe that he privately maintained an uncritical devotion. Later he recounted ironically that the Russian analyst Vera Schmidt had told him that the collectively raised children in her school manifested no Oedipus complex. When Fenichel asked her husband what the children called him, he replied "Papa." For Fenichel this sufficed to refute her claim (LI/15 October 1938/9).

The diffuseness of Fenichel's political pronouncements signal a quality of his entire oeuvre. His own methodology subordinated naked political declarations to quiet research. Fenichel affirmed that in every way Marxism and psychoanalysis were both scientific disciplines; they employed the scientific method; they were rigorous; and they also convinced fellow scientists by verifiable principles and results. Consequently, Marxist psychoanalysts need not shout their political beliefs when solid and productive work would more effectively demonstrate to the skeptics the validity of their perspective. By proceeding in this manner, the political Freudians would be confronting skepticism in the same way Freud had met disbelief.

As a methodology or tactic this approach bifurcated Fenichel's work. On the one hand, he was unambiguously devoted to a political psychoanalysis; on the other, he continuously made psychoanalytic contributions which barely breathed of politics. In his Berlin years he made a name for himself as a clear-eyed compiler and arbiter of psychoanalytic knowledge; but these contributions did not cross over into Marxism. At times the two endeavors touched; in his main psychoanalytic writings he regularly commented on and alluded to the social and political realities, but nothing more. He was content to show that psychoanalysis by itself was incomplete and required a sociology.

This tension or theoretical juggling is evident in the two main works he published in Berlin in 1931, *Perversionen, Psychosen, Charakterstoerungen* and *Hysterien und Zwangsneurosen,* the first of the textbooks which established his reputation. (They were published together in English as *Outline of Clinical Psychoanalysis*.) The introduction to the first volume touched on the historical parameters of neurosis, sharply attacking biologization. It is "false" and "dangerous" to believe that neurosis originates in the biological situation of the child. Not the Oedipus complex itself, but specific experiences give rise to neurosis; and these experiences rest on historical bases, for instance, the conduct of parents and teachers. Consequently neuroses change as do the social and moral structures of society. Here psychology proves its incompetence; the etiology of neurosis is not an "individual medical concern, but requires a sociological component. How could something like the Oedipus complex be fully understood without consideration of the history and function of the family?"

Fenichel broached the social and historical issue in the introduction precisely because he dropped it in the text. These points are discussed here, he indicates, "because in the following pages very little will be said of them, and nevertheless they must not be forgotten." They will not be pursued, he explains, because they remain the "darkest" area of psychoanalysis; moreover, the individual doctor is impotent to effect "social change." He or she can at best help individuals.[50] Only at the end of the second volume, which takes up character disorders, does Fenichel reopen the social issues. He did, however, devote the *Rundbriefe*, which he began in exile, to these "darkest" areas.

# CHAPTER FOUR

# Exile: The Secret
# Freudians and
# Their *Rundbriefe*

ON 30 January 1933 President Hindenburg appointed Adolf
Hitler chancellor of Germany. Within four weeks fire destroyed the German parliament, the Reichstag, and triggered
the suppression of Jews, leftists, and dissenters. For those arrested the Nazis set up what Hermann Göring labeled "concentration camps." In March Heinrich Himmler founded a
"model" camp at Dachau. By Christmas 1933 the camps contained some 27,000 internees.

These events initiated flight and panic among Jews and
leftists. Three-fourths of those who fled in 1933 settled close
to Germany, anticipating an early return. Lucy Dawidowicz
explains: "Sensible people were sure that Hitler could not last
long, that decency, rationality, and political order would—
must—reassert themselves."[1] Especially for those in the mid-

dle of their lives and careers, the decision to pick up and leave was protracted and wrenching. Hannah Tillich, the wife of Paul Tillich, recalled the "exhausting debates" among friends.

Paulus had to decide whether he could stay without endangering his own life and, even more important, the lives of his friends in the political underground. We walked the asphalt streets of the big city for hours. . . . The verdict was "Go". . . . We said farewell to a friend who poured us a glass of wine. . . . He had fetched his very best to honor us and our farewell. We drank a toast, "To overcome things to come." Our host committed suicide the following night.[2]

Leftists were the first to leave; official anti-Semitism propelled Jews to depart; by May 1933 book burnings that included Freud's works prompted psychoanalysts to exit. Wilhelm Reich set up headquarters in Copenhagen, which was also George Gero's destination. Fenichel escaped to Oslo, where he spent two years before moving to Prague. Friedländer and Lantos departed for Paris and later moved to London. Annie Reich fled to Prague. Edith Jacobson did not want to abandon her patients; she conferred with Gero in Copenhagen. Against his advice she returned to Germany and her patients where she was eventually arrested.

The expulsion from Central Europe gave psychoanalysis a fright from which it never recovered. That psychoanalysis prospered in exile, particularly in the United States, masked the injury; its most audacious theoreticians never recaptured the momentum of the pre-Hitler years. From the hour of exile, a conceptual retreat commenced. Analysts scrambling for visas and entry permits were in no position to boldly advance psychoanalysis. After 1933 psychoanalysis proceeded under the cloud of conservatism.

This conservatism represented not solely a political disposition, but more a wave of caution that passed through the psychoanalytic profession. Analysts did not have the time, energy, or inclination to challenge the psychoanalytic establishment. Nor was this retreat simply spontaneous. In 1934, certainly with the approval, and perhaps by the initiative of Freud, the International Psychoanalytic Association expelled Wilhelm Reich, its most prominent left-wing member. In the small analytic world, the lesson was not lost: psychoanalysis and radical politics do not mix.

The political Freudians organized themselves under these hostile conditions; they faced the inhospitality of the psychoanalytic profession and the inhospitality of the Western democracies toward radical Central European exiles. The formation of Fenichel's circle as a secret group must be understood within this context. From the start they were an embattled group, not even internally in accord with one another. Indeed their first task was to work out with Wilhelm Reich and his followers an agreement on a common program. When an agreement was not reached, the Fenichel people came together as their own group devoted to a political psychoanalysis.

The onset of nazism intensified opposite tendencies within psychoanalysis; some analysts moved forward to a more political posture while others retreated to a nonpolitical stance. For political, and recently exiled, analysts the palpable reality of victorious fascism spurred efforts to draw out the social implications of psychoanalysis. Reich immediately founded a new journal for "political psychology." With some help from Fenichel, he wrote the first issue almost totally by himself. An editorial note captured Reich's militancy; it announced that the magazine sought a Marxist economist as a contributor, but neither revisionists nor reformists should apply.[3]

In contrast, nazism hardened the resolve of the psychoanalytic establishment to stay out of politics. With the disintegration of the Berlin Institute, the mantle of psychoanalysis returned to Vienna and Freud. The Viennese analysts, responsive to Freud, not only argued that psychoanalysis and socialism were incompatible, but also that a political psycho-analysis was dangerous. They believed that if psychoanalysis maintained a low and nonpolitical profile it might escape sup-pression. Obviously these two tendencies clashed; the conflict resulted in the exclusion of Reich from the official analytic organization and in the formation of Fenichel's secret circle.

As the political Freudians regrouped in exile, they sought a common program on which to unify. As an organization they might nudge the psychoanalytic movement to the left. By virtue of his past achievements, his inexhaustible energy, and his magnetic personality, leadership of the group almost auto-matically belonged to Reich.[4] For six years (1924–30) in Vienna Reich conducted with Freud's implicit approval a much celebrated seminar on therapy; his *Character Analysis* (1933) set forth a very influential theory of character structure. From the late 1920s he had been championing the rapproche-ment of Marxism and psychoanalysis, with his "Dialectical Materialism and Psychoanalysis" representing the fullest ac-count of the subject to that date. He also immersed himself in the practical politics of sexual reform. With several other left-wing analysts in Vienna, he had opened clinics under the auspices of a Socialist Society for Sexual Advice and Sexual Research.

In Berlin, Reich's activities had increased. Inspired by Bro-nislaw Malinowski's anthropological work he wrote a book on the origins of sexual repression *(The Invasion of Compulsory Sex-Morality)*. Under the rubric of an association of "proletarian sexual politics" he unified separate groups devoted to sexual reform. He founded his own press, which eventually published his *Mass Psychology of Fascism*, perhaps his most salient work,[5] and he assumed leadership of left-wing analytic groups and discussions. He also joined the Communist party, where his duties were hardly revolutionary. The party assigned him to the same cell as Arthur Koestler. According to Koestler the cell went canvassing door-to-door: "We sold the World Revolution like vacuum cleaners."[6]

Indisputably Reich was a commanding and energetic figure in the psychoanalytic movement; even his opponents conceded he was brilliant, if misguided. Reich greatly impressed Freud until Reich turned to Marxism. Reich claimed that his own lecture on the prevention of neuroses provoked Freud's *Civilization and Its Discontents* with its sharp attack on Marxism. "I was the one," he said, who was "discontented" with civilization.[7] The session in which Reich forcefully presented his ideas to the Vienna Society constituted the single instance in which Richard F. Sterba, a Viennese analyst, witnessed Freud behaving as an angry authoritarian.[8]

To be sure, Reich was difficult and contentious, and he was unable to unify the political Freudians. Eventually the group split up. One segment followed Reich, and their story is almost synonymous with Reich's biography; another segment rallied to Fenichel, and their story is unknown.

It might seem surprising that Fenichel galvanized a circle to challenge Reich. In 1933 Reich's public and political identity far overshadowed Fenichel's. Yet among the other left-wing analysts, Fenichel was the most prominent. (Siegfried Bernfeld momentarily removed himself from the network, since he had earlier sided with Freud against Reich.[9]) Fenichel had conducted the Children's Seminar for ten years, and this had brought him in contact with all the younger and more political analysts. He had published a respected survey of psychoanalysis, and he was much acclaimed for his lucidity and command of analytic knowledge. If not in theoretical verve or originality, in discipline, energy, and intellect Reich met his match in Fenichel.

Reich and Fenichel's backgrounds were almost identical; they seemed destined to collaborate or conflict. They were born the same year (1897); both their fathers were Jews from

Galicia who strongly identified with German culture;[10] and both had a single brother. Both attended the Faculty of Medicine of the University of Vienna and they received their medical degrees a year apart (in 1921 and 1922).[11] In their early twenties, both delivered papers to the Vienna Psychoanalytic Society. Both conducted highly regarded seminars for many years (Reich's Seminar for Psychoanalytic Therapy and Fenichel's Children's Seminar). In addition, through Fenichel, Reich met his first wife, Annie Pink.

During 1933 and 1934 the political Freudians tried to hammer out a unified program for an "opposition" within the psychoanalytic movement. Reich and Fenichel had each fled to Scandanavia. There they participated in meetings in which they presented positions and tactics. After expulsion from Denmark and Sweden, Reich moved to Oslo in October 1934, where Fenichel had settled. Fenichel left Oslo for Prague approximately one year later. This signaled the final breach between them and the consolidation of the Fenichel circle.

The antagonisms that divided Reich and Fenichel's circles were certainly personal as well as theoretical and political. The validity of the personal charges is difficult to assess. In his autobiography Reich concludes that Fenichel was unfit for the rigors of a Marxist opposition and that Fenichel had laid a "trap" in assuming leadership.

"I naively believed that Fenichel had meant what he promised," when he undertook leadership and declared his solidarity; but, Reich asserts, Fenichel sought personal power. He refused to acknowledge Reich's contributions. "Fenichel usurped my findings, but tried to kill my theory with silence." His own success with patients, Reich believes, threatened Fenichel. Finally, he charges that Fenichel spread rumors of Reich's mental illness.[12]

Neither Fenichel's writings nor the *Rundbriefe* devote much space to these personal issues. However, many of Reich's sympathizers recognized his prickly temperament. "Already in those days [the early 1930s] only absolutes were possible for him," wrote Ilse Reich, his third wife. "You were for him or against him. . . . And those close to him had to follow or get out." Ilse Reich did not accept the belief of Annie Reich, his first wife, that Wilhelm suffered a mental deterioration beginning in the late 1920s.[13]

Fenichel's group seemed to have shared a belief in Reich's mental instability. In 1933 Fenichel and Edith Gyömröi traveled to Copenhagen for one of the frequent meetings they had with Reich to work out a program. She recalls:

We met Reich and went to the beach, talking endlessly as we walked. Reich, who meant very much to us at the time, told us about the outline of the book he was then working on. It was the beginning of his Orgon theory. Fenichel and I did not dare to look at each other, and had cold shivers. Then Reich suddenly stopped, and said: *"Kinder, wenn ich meiner Sache nicht so sicher wäre, würde es mich anmuten wie eine Skizophrene Fantasie"* ["Children, if I were not so certain of what I am working on, it would appear to me as a schizophrenic fantasy"]. We didn't say anything. Not even on our journey back. It was for us both a great loss and a great sorrow.[14]

There is no need to overemphasize or avoid the issue. Fenichel and other political Freudians became convinced that Reich was suffering a psychic break, and this was the prime reason for the formation of a separate circle of analysts. Unpublished memoirs and recollections reveal fairly widespread agreement about Reich's psychic condition,[15] the validity of which will not be weighed here. Yet the same recollections and memoirs often reiterated that Reich remained a man of incredible personal magnetism and force. After he moved to Oslo, he gained a devoted following, whereas Fenichel was unable to garner Norwegian supporters and for this reason departed for Prague.[16]

## Exile: The Secret Freudians and Their *Rundbriefe*

It is important to consider that Reich's mental condition may have been caused or exacerbated by his catastrophic situation. Reich was the Job of the psychoanalytic movement, assaulted from every direction. He summarized his plight telegraphically: "Collapse on all fronts, disappointment in former bulwarks, as well as serious personal troubles."[17] At the time of his exile, his marriage to Annie Reich ended; she proceeded with the children to Prague, and he initially moved to Copenhagen. Insofar as Annie Reich became part of the Fenichel circle, it is likely that this embittered and compounded his antagonism toward Fenichel.

The setbacks that Reich suffered might unhinge anyone. In 1933 as he fled Berlin the psychoanalytic establishment was already preparing to purge him. He first stopped in Vienna, where he was invited to drop out of the Psychoanalytic Association; he was also instructed to "refrain from lecturing or debating in political meetings—particularly communist ones—here in Austria."[18] His book, *Character Analysis,* was in page proofs when the official psychoanalytic press, evidently following Freud's command, rescinded its acceptance, forcing Reich to publish it himself.[19] Ironically it contained no explicit politics. Today many analysts believe it is an indispensable work.[20]

Nor did Reich's situation improve once he left Vienna. In Denmark, his first place of exile, he was harassed and finally denied residency. There was a suit filed against a journal that published an article by Reich claiming the article pornographic, although it had appeared previously in a German psychoanalytic journal. A press campaign was launched against the infamous Berlin sexologist. When Freud was asked to defend Reich publicly, he refused. Reich fled to Sweden where the situation was replicated; he was harassed and denied residency. Almost simultaneously he was expelled from both the Communist party and—an especially grievous blow—from the International Psychoanalytic Association. A biographer concludes: "Within eighteen months he had been excluded from three countries, from the Danish Communist Party (which he had never joined), and from the Psychoanalytic Association."[21] If Reich lost his mental equilibrium, he had sufficient cause.

On this swamp of defeats and rejections, Reich and Fenichel tried to lay the groundwork for an alliance of oppositional psychoanalysts. The expulsion of Reich from the International Association (Lucerne Congress, August 1934) intensified these efforts. Reich, Fenichel, and other political Freudians regularly gathered in order to establish common principles. This opposition would rally to Reich and generally devote itself to issues germane to a political psychoanalysis. However, sharp differences divided the group; the negotiations resulted in a break between Reich and Fenichel and the commencement of the *Rundbriefe.*

In Reich's version of these events, Fenichel never rose to the historic occasion; he failed to galvanize a public group that would forcefully defend Reich. Rather, according to Reich, Fenichel fudged issues, vacillated, and retreated; he feared sharing Reich's fate, expulsion from the psychoanalytic organization. Reich said of him:

The true reason is that he never intended to risk exclusion at all. However, he should have come out and said so, instead of hiding behind the excuse that first of all one had to have greater influence. How? By avoiding all controversy, by soft-peddling one's own work.[22]

Fenichel in the *Rundbriefe* described a talk of Reich's in which he denounced Fenichel. Reich reiterated that he was "completely alone" at the Lucerne Congress, and that Fenichel had refused to criticize Freud directly, not wishing to get expelled. Fenichel partly agreed saying, "The most important thing that I can do now for the psychoanalytic movement is not to get myself thrown out." Reich also claimed that Fenichel understood very little of the issues, and added that he, Reich, had actually initiated Fenichel's circle in Berlin. Since his own political activity consumed so much time, he had asked Fenichel to keep other analysts informed, and these analysts became Fenichel's group (XI/2 February 1935/1).

Reich later summarized his position:

Fenichel did not understand that it was not a question of a few persons who, as friends, began an opposition movement. He did not understand that it was not a matter of personal considerations, but that what was called for was a clear formulation of some decisive basic issues. He tried to lead the opposition in such a way that, as far as possible, no one should learn of its existence. It should be *"Secret."* The opposition should be "Marxist analysts."[23]

Reich was accurate about the secrecy. Fenichel and his circle had wanted to avoid a direct confrontation with the psychoanalytic establishment, and they did maintain a secret group. Whether personal timidity predominated is open to question. Fenichel responded to Reich. "I believe, to be sure, that it cannot be kept secret that we correspond and exchange opinions with one another." However, he continued, the manner in which our exchanges take place; "who takes part in it and what opinions are expressed" must be kept secret.[24]

To cast the characters as the "forthright" Reich and the "cautious" Fenichel would falsify the reality. Reich demanded an opposition based exclusively on his own theoretical work, namely his orgasm theory. He even objected to calling the group Marxist.[25] "There was no other program than mine for an opposition movement."[26] A lecture Fenichel delivered in Oslo, stating that since Freud's *Three Contributions* nothing important had been written on sexuality, provoked Reich. "He had forgotten my orgasm theory." This was no minor matter; to Reich "historically all differences evolved precisely around this question."[27] For Reich there was only one way to go, and Fenichel declined. "Fenichel never wanted to commit himself unequivocally to my scientific program." Reich included in this program his orgasm theory as well as the notions of "sex-economy" and "sex-politics," which have "points of contact with psychoanalysis," but form "an independent field."[28]

Fenichel increasingly found Reich's theories less acceptable. He wrote in the *Rundbriefe*,

Regarding Reich's letter, it is agreed that a platform from which we can carry on our opposition work must definitely be worked out. . . . Such a platform ought *not* to contain comprehensive concepts such as the Reichian concept regarding the death instinct and anxiety, in which one had to believe dogmatically.[29]

Fenichel did not unconditionally rally to Reich's ideas for at least two reasons: he did not sufficiently agree with them, and he did not believe they were broad enough to unify an opposition. Reich, on the other hand, maintained it as self-evident that a group must swear allegiance to his theories.

Since Reich was becoming ever more difficult, and since he was demanding unconditional subordination to a theory that was rapidly leaving behind both psychoanalysis and Marxism, friends and students found themselves hard pressed to support him. Fenichel chose to lead a covert group of analysts who could not completely accept Reich's theories; who were unwilling openly to challenge the official psychoanalytic organization; and who were dedicated to exploring the issues of a social and political psychoanalysis.

The *Rundbriefe* signified Fenichel's unflagging effort to sustain this group of analysts and sustain the idea of a political psychoanalysis. "Despite all obstacles," he wrote in an early letter, "these Rundbriefe are necessary for the union of analysts of our orientation." He did not "exaggerate" the importance of their small circle; however, their group might make contact with a "larger circle." Among themselves they would circulate raw unedited contributions, manuscripts "for house use." The group would function as a "written Children's Seminar of Marxist psychoanalysis." Gradually it would reach out. He begged everyone to send in notices and information, distilled from their own correspondence, which would be relevant to their project. (XI/12 February 1935/3–5). Theoretically their political psychoanalysis would run up against both the professional analysts and the professional politicians or Marxists. As he explained sometime later to Arnold Zweig, their group was "constantly fighting against two fronts"—against analysts who had no appreciation of the social reality and against Marxists who had no appreciation of individual reality (?XXIX/7 July 1936/14).

For eleven and a half years without missing a beat, through several exiles, Fenichel, every three to six weeks, typed out these letters with at least six carbons and sent them out to the six analysts. He meticulously corrected the typing mistakes in each carbon. The sheer labor of typing, correcting, and colating testifies to Fenichel's supreme discipline and devotion.

Recipients responded directly to Fenichel, and he cited or excerpted their responses in subsequent *Rundbriefe*. Since Fenichel maintained a massive correspondence outside the *Rundbriefe*, he frequently cited from these letters and reports; for personal or political reasons he rarely identified the author of this material. He simply stated that he received news about the psychoanalytic situation in London or Chicago as well as Brazil, Argentina, and Romania. He also cited "third person" letters—letters neither to nor from himself—which someone else had passed along.

The exchanges presupposed secrecy; only in this way could an uninhibited discussion of issues and people flourish. Often Fenichel counseled the others to maintain "extreme discretion and care" with the letters (XVII/30 August 1935/10). On occasion he suggested they burn the letters after reading them. "One should not forget how unpleasant it would be if these *Rundbriefe* fell into the wrong hands! . . . For that reason I have asked that they be burnt after reading. Whoever does not want to do that, has to at least handle them so carefully that no one uninvited can see them" (XXIII/3 March 1936/13). Between this advice and the exigencies of exile, few copies exist.

Internally the letters followed no plan. Insofar as they served as a theoretical sounding board and as a lifeline for analysts, the length and contents of the sections and letters widely differed. Long debates or lectures or reviews filled some sections, while others briefly reported news such as announcements of publications or short accounts of activities. (See the appendix for an outline of four sample *Rundbriefe*.)

The *Rundbriefe* provide a gold mine of information about psychoanalytic events, history, and theory. Fenichel kept tabs on who was where, what courses and lectures were being delivered, and what were the current disputes. He gave detailed accounts of all the psychoanalytic congresses, especially those from Marienbad to Chicago that he attended. He maintained a running commentary on the organizational decisions of the International Psychoanalytic Association and, later, when in the United States, of the American Psychoanalytic Association.

He seemed to have read everything. He regularly listed and commented on psychoanalytic literature in the *Rundbriefe*, especially if it had any bearing on social or political issues. While living in Prague, for instance, Fenichel summarized articles on psychoanalysis that appeared in the *American Journal of Sociology*. He sometimes included his own lengthy reviews of books ranging from works by Freud *(Moses and Monotheism);* to books on Marxism and psychoanalysis (Bartlett's

*Marxism and Psychoanalysis)* and subjects distant from psychoanalysis (Arnold's *Folklore of Capitalism*). He offered advice and information. To those seeking entry to the United States, he once typed out a three-page model of a curriculum vitae.

The early *Rundbriefe* regularly returned to the subject of Reich. Fenichel included countless items about Reich: reviews of recent publications; reports on activities; and accounts of the machinations of the psychoanalytic establishment. A rough continuity guided the Fenichel people in regards to Reich. Although they remained sympathetic to the core of his work, this sympathy weakened as he revised his own theories; and although they made a clean break with any personal collaboration, they continued to defend Reich against official psychoanalysis.

Fenichel cited in the *Rundbriefe* a lengthy letter by an analyst of his group who had abandoned Reich's circle; the letter was directed to Reich and expressed the position of the Fenichel people. This analyst explained that he refused an organizational connection to Reich. Yet he was not an enemy but a friend. "It is only your fixed idea that anyone who does not completely agree, is an enemy." He was unwilling to "swear" allegiance to character analysis and sexual economy.

However, I had the impression in Oslo that discussion is no longer very easy with you. It seems that an atmosphere dominates in which scientific discussion can hardly prosper. An opponent—and everyone is an opponent who does not believe in advance—is hardly heard, since it is supposed that he is wrong and must knuckle under. That is apparently the position towards Fenichel.

Much can be learned from Fenichel, the analyst continued, and Reich's continual denigration of Fenichel is reprehensible, proof of the impossibility of discourse. On at least one issue

Fenichel is "completely right": Reich's phenomenological description of orgasm is incomplete. Neurotic symptoms disturb sexuality, not simply vice versa (XIII/4 April 1935/4).

While Fenichel himself did not reject Reich's contribution to psychoanalysis, he distanced himself more and more from what he considered its simplifications. He sympathetically reviewed Reich's *Mass Psychology of Fascism*, but he questioned whether Reich's critique of economic reductionism risked the opposite error, sexual reductionism. Reich exploded sexuality into its historical and economic components, but his "sexual politics" surrendered his own insights. When Reich imagined that "by some kind of 'sexual politics' all humanity can be lead directly to heaven or at least into revolutionary action," he exaggerated the sexual remedy.[30] With mounting concern Fenichel reviewed Reich's publications in the *Rundbriefe*. He failed to understand what Reich's "muscle analysis" or "vegetative therapy" offered to analysis. After reading a new essay by Reich ("Experimental Investigation of the Electrical Function of Sexuality and Anxiety"[31]) Fenichel concluded that it could not be seriously accepted. "Marxist analysts" must "silently reject" it (XXXVI/? May 1937/13).

In a series of lectures given in Vienna in 1936 (and published in English as *Problems of Psychoanalytic Technique*) Fenichel declared his agreement "in essentials" with Reich's *Character Analysis,* though he again noted Reich's penchant for "schematic simplification." Since publication of that book, however, Reich "has undergone an unsatisfactory development which has led him entirely away from psychoanalysis."[32] In 1937 Fenichel expressed his complete accord with the opinion of another analyst: "Reich's themes are very exaggerated. Reich himself is monotonous or completely *meschugge*. Some of his theories are surely very interesting, indeed ingenious, but in the main, rational men must repudiate them" (XXXIV/17 March 1937/8).

# Exile: The Secret Freudians and Their *Rundbriefe*

Despite these grave theoretical and political differences Fenichel defended Reich, although with insufficient vigor to appease him. When the Viennese psychoanalytic establishment attacked Reich, Fenichel came to his aid. This was fitting since pronouncements by the Viennese enjoyed a special status; the presence of Freud conferred on their statements a stamp of legitimacy and orthodoxy.

In 1934 Robert Waelder, a Viennese analyst and co-editor of *Imago*,[33] evaluated Reich's new journal. His review extended far beyond the journal to a general assessment of Reich's career and contributions. On the heels of Reich's expulsion from the international association, a statement by a Viennese editor of an approved psychoanalytic journal smacked of an official statement.

Waelder harbored no sympathy for a political or Marxist psychoanalysis; he argued that it was illegitimate to mix science (psychoanalysis) and politics. Waelder justified his discoursing on politics and psychoanalysis by the fact that Wilhelm Reich, who had served psychoanalysis well, especially through clinical work, now promoted a political psychoanalysis. According to Waelder, past contributions do not sanction present activities. He closed by stating "It must be said in all clarity, that this 'scientific' effort [of Reich's] has nothing more to do with psychoanalysis; and no one who follows Reich on his path has the right to appeal to psychoanalysis."[34]

Reich himself judged the Waelder review to be the official statement of his expulsion, especially since no other reasons appeared in print. Fenichel had published an essay in this same journal of Reich's,[35] and inasmuch as Waelder did not mention Fenichel in his general attack on Reich and the journal, Reich inferred that Fenichel had collaborated with the psychoanalytic authorities.[36] Rejecting that inference as absurd, Fenichel wrote that Reich's allegation reminded him of the story of the German worker who said to the Jewish socialist agitator: " 'You are a Jew; you have it easy since the Jews all stick together'; and the Jew replied, 'Oy, how the rich Jews stick with me!' " (XVII/30 August 1935/3).

In fact Fenichel had already drafted a reply which supported Reich; he circulated the reply in the *Rundbriefe*, where it was discussed, and he submitted it to Waelder for publication in *Imago*. Fenichel declared that "many colleagues" shared Reich's commitment to Marxism, and indeed Fenichel would be curious to learn why Marxism was incompatible with psychoanalysis. He also corrected some of Waelder's statements about Marxism (XII/? March 1935/3).

After a long delay Waelder responded to Fenichel, inaugurating a series of exchanges between Fenichel and official Vienna. Waelder apologized for the late response, explaining that Fenichel's letter had caused "great embarrassment." The decision as to whether to publish the rebuttal was extremely difficult, and so as not to bear the sole responsibility, he had invited Ernst Kris, the other editor, to join him. In the near future he and Kris would officially notify Fenichel as to why it was impossible to publish his rebuttal. Nevertheless Waelder elaborated for several pages what he had meant to say in his review; he regretted some infelicities which may have given rise to misunderstandings. He also made the "request" that Fenichel withdraw his rebuttal (XVI/6 June 1935/1).

Fenichel never seemed to have received the official rejection, but he responded to this unofficial letter. He did not give an inch. He stated at the outset that he saw no reason to accede to the request to withdraw his rebuttal, which would only free Waelder from the responsibility of rejecting it. Waelder's review demanded a response insofar as it gave rise to the "suspicion that the review presents an official statement" of the International Psychoanalytic Association. The fact that the public statement that had been promised on Reich's expulsion had not been issued reinforced the suspicion. Fenichel wrote that he agreed that the reason for the expulsion

"We consider Reich too pathological" is not publishable; but that should not be replaced by another which falsely states that Reich's Marxism is incompatible with psychoanalysis; in this case, colleagues, who are in accord with Reich *on this point*, get the impression that they are not wanted in the International Association. (XVI/6 June 1935/1)

Two conclusions may be drawn about this exchange. Fenichel continued to defend Reich and the project of a political psychoanalysis; and Waelder and the Viennese analysts were extremely eager to mollify Fenichel. In fact, the exchanges did not end with Fenichel's counterreply. Waelder continued to justify, explain, and inquire—though he did not concede. At the same time, he rejected for publication Fenichel's "The Drive to Amass Wealth."[37] Yet the Viennese were making a very determined effort to keep Fenichel within the fold. Why?

It would be difficult, without more documentation, to determine the precise attitudes of the Viennese analysts toward Reich and Fenichel. As Reich's Marxism became more open and aggressive, it is clear that Freud turned decisively against him. It must be remembered that Reich was not just an able analyst of the second generation, but in the 1920s his clinical work, his seminars, and his writings also marked him as outstanding, perhaps the very best of his generation. Hence the "loss" of Reich to Marxism and to other pursuits was painful to the Viennese guardians of psychoanalysis.

It seems likely that they were anxious to avoid a similar situation with Fenichel. Like Reich, Fenichel was more than an able psychoanalyst; he commanded a prodigious amount of information; he wrote well and often; he incisively commented on theoretical matters; and he kowtowed to no one. Fenichel was a force to be reckoned with. Psychoanalysis could not afford to lose its most talented practitioners. Freud's own role in the politicking is unclear, but it is certain he was not passive.[38] As a whole the Vienna group worked to retain good relations with Fenichel.

Evidence of these efforts can be gleaned from Fenichel's trip to Vienna and from the fact the Viennese solicited a major essay from Fenichel. Not long after the exchange with Waelder, Fenichel left Oslo for Prague, visiting several cities en route. In Vienna he met with several analysts, among them Bergler, Kris, Lampl, Federn, and Waelder. Fenichel rarely recorded personal impressions in the *Rundbriefe*, but in Vienna he discerned an attitude of deference toward himself: "One had the feeling that they all feared me a little" (?XIX/17 October 1935/6).

Fenichel had directed a letter to Edward Bibring and Ernst Kris that addressed the "crisis" and disarray of contemporary psychoanalysis. This letter formed the basis of a lengthy discussion between Fenichel and the editors of *Imago* and the *Internationale Zeitschrift für Psychoanalyse* (Kris, Waelder, Bibring, Hartmann). After this discussion, the editors conferred with Freud; according to Kris, this was the first editorial meeting with Freud in three years. With Freud's "complete agreement," they returned with an offer: Fenichel should write a brochure, a critical overview of present psychoanalytic knowledge (XX/23 November 1935/2). Fenichel borrowed the language of Marxism to explain its terms: he and the Vienna group would constitute a "united front." They would bury internal differences (on the death instinct, for example) and join hands against common enemies: the pernicious impact of Melanie Klein, Ferenczi, and American psychoanalysis.

By title and conception Fenichel's work was patterned on previous psychoanalytic surveys: "Report on the Progress of Psychoanalysis in the Years 1909–1913,"[39] and *Report on the*

*Progress of Psychoanalysis 1914–1919.*[40] Both were collective projects. Since the last report, which included essays by Rank, Ferenczi, and Theodor Reik, nothing similar had appeared. Both Fenichel and the Vienna group viewed "Progress of Psychoanalysis 1930–1936," Fenichel's working title, as a major confrontation with current psychoanalysis. That Freud and the Vienna group were willing to entrust to a single author a project that took several analysts to handle when the discipline was much smaller, suggests their confidence in Fenichel.

Nevertheless, the group had raised a question about Fenichel that concerned not his command of the material, but his politics. In the preliminary discussions of the project the Viennese feared that Fenichel's survey might be excessively critical and partisan. Kris had pointed out the danger of a report on psychoanalytic "progress" that would harp on the regressions. Freud himself shared Kris's fears, and communicated to Fenichel, through the Viennese editors, that "one must give a hearing to other standpoints." He obliquely cautioned Fenichel to avoid describing "too much the details of the water stains on the wall, instead of showing where the leak is" (XIX/17 October 1935/1). Finally he suggested that Fenichel avoid all polemics and crudities.

Disquiet on this score continued to mar the negotiations. Fenichel submitted a partial draft. The editors responded very positively; they deemed it "extraordinarily *impressive.*" They did, however, raise a number of criticisms and suggestions, some minor and some not so minor. They reminded Fenichel of some material he had skipped; and, more pointedly, they questioned the "tone" of the draft. They asked him to render his own standpoint "more objective." "That does not mean that you must renounce criticisms, but concerns exclusively the placing of accent and emphasis" (XXIII/3 March 1936/3).

Fenichel was pleased to include the omitted material, but

the advice to moderate or deemphasize his critique rankled him. He wrote the four editors:

It is my conviction that contemporary psychoanalysis requires a critique; and that is the reason for this work. I do not intend a long-winded polemic or to bicker over details; rather I intend to present my position "objectively"—where possible. In general a critical spirit informs the principal contents of the entire work (XXIII/3 March 1936/3).

Unfortunately, the available papers reveal nothing more of the project. The work was never published, and it survives only as an incomplete manuscript. It seems likely that the Viennese editors and Fenichel reached an impasse; it is also possible that other realities—the exigencies of exile life—intervened to prevent its publication or completion.

The existing manuscript begins by noting that a neutral compilation of psychoanalytic research in the style of the earlier reports would no longer be useful; the extent and disarray of present psychoanalytic knowledge suggest that "not only order but a critique is necessary." The manuscript surveys the literature on ego psychology, and goes on to criticize Melanie Klein at length.

Fenichel attacks her on several counts: that her case histories lacked substance; that she bypassed the daily or actual lives of her patients as if she could directly enter into the unconscious; that she ascribed too many psychic events to the Oedipus complex, which then becomes a blank category; and that she applies the language appropriate for later developmental phases too facilely to earlier phases. He does, however, credit Klein with the discovery of the destructive object tendencies of earliest childhood. In general Fenichel concludes that the English analysts suffered from "an exaggeration of biology." They relegated the "social moment" of neurosis to the background. It cannot be doubted that defenses originate in physiological helplessness; but the later defenses are not explained when they are traced back to the first situation. "Neuroses—and this is exactly the discovery of psychoanalysis—are the consequences of experiences."[41]

The breakdown of Fenichel's negotiations with Vienna over his critique anticipated the future. His links to official psychoanalysis frayed, although they never snapped. The political Freudians turned inward to stoke the theoretical fires; they exchanged manuscripts, ideas, and projects, but little intruded into the wider psychoanalytic community. As exile became not temporary but permanent, they retrenched. They surrendered the hope of a political psychoanalysis by settling to defend classical analysis in its full breadth and depth.

# CHAPTER FIVE

# Psychoanalysis and Its Discontents: Freudians Against Freudians

FENICHEL kept his circle informed of his negotiations with Vienna and of its psychoanalytic activities, since he regularly journeyed to Vienna from Prague. Among these activities was the celebration in 1936 of Freud's eightieth birthday, which lasted several days and included innumerable congratulatory lectures.[1] Ernest Jones, who opened the festivities, asserted that the era of German psychoanalysis was past; the English speaking lands now assumed the lead. An incredulous Fenichel commented that the talk following Jones's by Mrs. Riviere, an English Kleinian, effectively refuted this assessment; she was clear proof that England did not lead the psychoanalytic movement.

The lecture by Thomas Mann to honor Freud did not move Fenichel, who preferred the Mann of *Buddenbrooks*. Similarly the talk by Ludwig Binswanger, the existential almost theological analyst, left Fenichel cold. Binswanger spoke as if a church choir hung on his words. Fenichel recalled a comment by Freud: "Some people get drunk from wine; this Binswanger gets drunk without alcohol" (XXVI/18 March 1936/5). Freud, who did not attend, sent Binswanger a diplomatic note after reading the lecture: "I enjoyed your beautiful style, your erudition, the breadth of your horizon, your tact in contradicting me. . . . Of course, I don't believe you."[2]

The real issue, however, was the rising tide of fascism and the fate of psychoanalysis. By 1933, all psychoanalysis had not ceased in Germany; nor had all psychoanalysts fled. Many, including some who did depart, hoped that psychoanalysis might subsist under restricted conditions. Fenichel was keeping a running account of the German efforts to reconstruct the Berlin Institute and German psychoanalysis. He reported to his circle that, in the presence of Ernest Jones, the suggestion was aired to relegate Jews from the status of full members to "guests" of the German Society.[3]

Understandably the Fenichel group harbored little sympathy for a revamped Berlin Institute. In 1935 several from the circle received invitations from Felix Boehm, president of the German Society, asking them to send congratulations on the fifteenth anniversary of the Berlin Institute. Fenichel himself had spoken at the tenth anniversary, and Freud had written a preface to the volume published for the occasion. The situation in five years had changed. References to Freud in Institute publications were eliminated; Jews were not welcome. Even Boehm himself dabbled in Nazi ideas.[4] In response to the invitation, Edith Gyömröi cabled her greetings on behalf of the circle: "On the occasion of the fifteenth anniversary, former members think fondly of the old administration of free research and wish further prospering under the old flag" (XII/? March 1935/5).

The old flag had long since been retired. By June 1936 the break in the Berlin Institute between the Germans and the remaining Jews was complete. Fenichel monitored these events, although in reporting them he rarely indicated his sources. He later admitted that he and Edith Jacobson had been disastrously wrong in supposing that even a curtailed psychoanalysis could by preserved in Germany; it would have been much better simply to have dissolved the German Society in the spring of 1933, as Reich had proposed: "I must confess that at the time I and Edith Jacobson, in opposition to Reich, represented the contrary position" (XXXVI/? May 1937/5).

Yet the congenital obtuseness of the psychoanalytic establishment scandalized Fenichel; it was unable to apprehend the reality of nazism. On the day the Nazis marched into Vienna, Fenichel noted, the Viennese analysts were still behaving like "usual Viennese burgers: a short agitated panic followed by a great confidence in the present government." The refusal of the Austrian analysts to flee was compounded by their belief —not shared by Fenichel—that the "collapse of the Vienna group" entailed the "collapse of psychoanalysis generally" (XLIV/14 March 1938/4).

The inability or refusal to confront nazism proved costly to the psychoanalytic establishment; it failed to defend its material resources. Fenichel related a tale he found very instructive:

During the preparations for Freud's eightieth birthday something again happened which might open the eyes of the good analysts to the relationship between fascism and psychoanalysis and which demonstrates to us their continued blindness. Although it is now three years since Freud's books were burnt in Berlin, for these three long years the International Psychoanalytic Press left the bulk of its book stock in Leipzig. Now on the order of the regime the stock has been seized and ordered destroyed. The material loss for the press is extraordinarily large. It plans to lodge a complaint—in German courts! (XXVI/18 May 1936/4)

Jones later recounted, "I immediately cabled the Chief of Police in Leipzig explaining that it [the stock of books] belonged to an international body, but of course this did not deter their actions."[5]

The mounting pressure of fascism was felt everywhere, especially for the Fenichel group after Edith Jacobson was arrested in 1936. Fortunately she was incarcerated in a local prison. As she noted in a paper summarizing her experiences, "Observations on the Psychological Effect of Imprisonment on Female Political Prisoners," it was regulated more benignly than the concentration camps.[6] For months, plans circulated throughout the international psychoanalytic community and in the *Rundbriefe* on how to secure her release. She became quite ill and was temporarily freed so as to recover; at this point some of the Prague analysts helped smuggle her across the border to Czechoslovakia.

Jacobson's arrest intensified the anxiety of the Vienna analysts. Freud believed that the Austrian authorities would shield Austria and psychoanalysis from nazism. To avoid irritating the Austrians, the Vienna Society ruled in 1935 that analysts and candidates should not participate in illegal political activity. One leftist candidate, Marie Langer, later to emigrate to Argentina, ran afoul of the society; it almost expelled her after she was briefly arrested.[7] In view of the delicate political circumstances, however, Fenichel did not judge the Viennese restrictions especially onerous (XXVII/? 30 August 1936/5).

The encroaching fascism did not deflect the Fenichel circle from its primary commitment, the discussion of a social and political psychoanalysis. Indeed the group tried to turn exile into a theoretical advantage. One *Rundbriefe* recipient suggested that the refugees possessed a rare opportunity to compare patients and materials. Since they were now located in a half a dozen new cultures, they could reexamine with fresh material a recurring theme of political psychoanalysis, the relative weight of history and nature on psychological life: Are there national forms of character structure? Does character structure vary from culture to culture?

George Gero, living in Copenhagen, commenced the discussion. He did not doubt that the unconscious was "international," but the Scandinavian "character form" sharply differed from the German or Hungarian. He attributed this to divergent patterns of education and superego formation. In Hungary, for example, the typical petty bourgeois father might physically threaten his teenage daughter for violating sexual conventions. By contrast, in Scandinavia, the typical father gave his daughter much more freedom, but also burdened her with more responsibility, indicating that her parents would be gravely disappointed if she engaged in sexual activity. Obviously guilt and superego played a different role in the Scandinavian and Hungarian character structures (XII/? 11 March 1935/2).

Fenichel agreed with Gero, but he pointed to the dangers of a reductionism à la Géza Róheim that treated cultures as individuals, categorizing them as oral, anal, and genital types. Rather, the historical conditions of each country that shape national character structures should be investigated. Fenichel emphasized that the same instincts assume different forms depending on the fates they have suffered. History stamps neurosis with its insignia. In support of his contention, Fenichel referred to the fact that analysts at the time rarely came across the "classic" neurosis—hysteria. This he believed reflected the historical dynamic of neurosis. The progression of neuroses registered the progression of history; hysteria belonged to an earlier phase of social morality (XII/? 11 March 1935/2).

An unflagging awareness of biological and cultural reductionism marked Fenichel's contributions to all theoretical discussions. On every issue he distinguished his position from a biologism he associated with Róheim, Laforgue, Marie Bona-parte, and sometimes Jones and Freud; and he wanted to avoid the culturalism linked to Horney and Fromm. The same analysts, Fenichel noted, occasionally replaced one deficiency with the other. Michael Balint, a Hungarian disciple of Ferenczi, had leaned toward a biologism; after Ferenczi's death, however, he succumbed to the "opposite extreme," a sappy romanticism. Since Balint had been an ally, his new direction distressed Fenichel (XV/17 June 1935/17).

Balint had earlier sent Fenichel a manuscript, asking for comments. Following his usual procedure, Fenichel responded with a fifteen-page critique, which led to several additional exchanges. Fenichel fully agreed with Balint's rejection of biologism. For Fenichel Mrs. Riviere represented an "extreme" version of this "false direction" that ignored reality by defining psychoanalysis as exclusively a science of infantile fantasies. Nevertheless, Fenichel decried Balint's (new) neglect of the instinctual base of psychic life. In his interpretation of the stages of libido, Balint placed all his emphasis on education and the cultural world.

Fenichel closed his detailed and unyielding critique in good spirits: "Send me soon an anticritique!" Balint was not pleased; he rejoined acidly that if he were not an analyst "accustomed to dealing with resistances" he could not understand how an intelligent man like Fenichel could "so thoroughly escape the normal processes" of argument. Balint affirmed that they both agreed on the importance of social factors, conceding that he previously had neglected them. "It is, and remains the service of the 'Communist' wing (Reich & Fenichel & Co.) to have made us attentive to that." For the rest he was not convinced (XVII/30 August 1935/7).

Fenichel also maintained an exchange of manuscripts and letters with Balint's wife, Alice Balint. Her criticisms of Fenichel's manuscript, "The Drive to Amass Wealth" evolved into a discussion of the psychoanalytic uses of anthropology. Fenichel agreed with Alice Balint that he had not examined the origin of money, only its function; but he challenged her belief that additional anthropological field work would necessarily illuminate its origin. For Fenichel, Róheim's psychoanalytic anthropology unfortunately revealed that field work happily coexisted with deficient theorizing.

Alice Balint maintained that a crude determinism pervaded the old anthropological tradition on which Engels had based his work. "Against Marxists who are content with dogma," Fenichel concurred, it is necessary "to refer again and again to the necessity to studying real conditions" (XX/23 November 1935/4). Nevertheless he detected in Alice Balint the blight of culturalism; she exaggerated the role of education and accepted what Fenichel called "the swindel of personality." Paraphrasing Marx—and reversing his youthful formulations on education—Fenichel stated that "in capitalist society narrow limits are set on educational reforms." Society will not be changed by revolutionizing humanity through education, but by changing the social conditions (XXXVII/29 June 1937/5).

Against cultural optimism, Fenichel emphasized the biological, almost intractable, flow of psychic life. Yet he did not resolve the issue of the relative significance of culture and instinct. Indeed Fenichel's own formulations provoked dissent in the *Rundbriefe*. Recipients bandied about the theme of culturalism or what became designated "Rousseauism": man is naturally good but society is corrupt. Insofar as Rousseauism simplified to the point of falsehood the nature of desire, eros, and instincts, Fenichel, loyal to Freud, rejected it outright. However, Fenichel's own critique of the romantic illusion came perilously close to Freud's late pessimism; it almost accepted the opposite supposition: a natural aggression and evil renders man immune to cultural transformations.

Obviously political psychoanalysts could not accept this

proposition. As Freudians the group did not want to yield to vague ideas on the future resolution of neurosis and sexual antagonism; they resisted a culturalism or what they considered a reformism that failed to confront the psychic depths. Nevertheless several *Rundbriefe* recipients questioned whether Fenichel in rejecting culturalism overemphasized biology.

Two propositions that earned general assent were that the instinctual life of humanity is not accessible to shallow reforms, and that the instinctual life is not damned to eternal sameness. One recipient of the *Rundbriefe,* formerly a follower of Reich's, contributed: "There is only one correct answer to the question, what will the instinctual life of man be like after generations of socialist society? We do not know." However, he continued, clinical experience suggests that the cessation of sexual anxiety will produce an "incredible liberation." Socialism may not inaugurate paradise, but it will bring Utopia closer (?XXIV/? March 1936/9). While Fenichel agreed, he discerned hints of a Reichian sexual reductionism and romanticism in these statements. Sexual oppression, Fenichel replied, is a "consequence and instrument" of domination, but "only *one* consequence and instrument." Romanticism had distorted Reich's vision: an evil society corrupted a naturally benign sexuality; consequently, according to Fenichel, in Reich's schema the end of sexual repression initiated a life of joy.

These exchanges on romanticism and culture fed into a major theme that troubled the Fenichel circle, their relationship with the neo-Freudians. There were endless letters, reviews, and comments devoted to this issue. It was never resolved, and in large measure, the theoretical irresolution of the political Freudians hastened their demise. To the political Freudians, the neo-Freudians presented a hope and a threat. The conservatism and biologism of establishment psychoanalysis dissatisfied the neo-Freudians; to correct this imbalance, they introduced social and historical categories. Here they

crossed paths with the Fenichel group. However, in their eager-
ness to modernize psychoanalysis, they surrendered its critical
spirit, its dimensions of the unconscious and sexuality. Here
they parted from the Fenichel people.

Fenichel realized that his own position on the neo-Freudians
required a finely tuned theoretical ear and a pragmatic tactical
touch. The mixture was rare. Against the flat culturalism of the
neo-Freudians, Fenichel stressed the instinctual and sexual
depths. As a political Freudian, he also denounced biological
reductionism and the social blindness of mainstream psychoanalysis. For this reason he warmly greeted the neo-Freudians
as allies—only to criticize sharply their revisions. On this score
he sided with the psychoanalytic conservatives with whom he
shared little.

While Fenichel's position was theoretically coherent, even
stringent, in the midst of psychoanalytic squabbles it pleased
very few. As the neo-Freudians gathered support, the lines
hardened. The conservatives glued themselves to Freud's texts
and denounced a social or political psychoanalysis that built on
these texts. The neo-Freudians rejected by the conservatives
discarded more and more dimensions of psychoanalysis finally
embracing a very lax sociologism. Fenichel who saw the truth
in each position was welcomed by neither faction.

Abram Kardiner, for instance, wrote to Fenichel soliciting
a sympathetic review of his *Individual and His Society*. [8] With
bitterness, Kardiner complained that the New York analytic
establishment unanimously derided his attention to an anthropological psychoanalysis, judging that his work subverted
canonical psychoanalysis. Since Fenichel was "looked upon as
a champion of conservatism," a friendly review might turn the
tide (LX/11 August 1939/9).

Fenichel bridled at Kardiner's label: "I don't think that my
point of view in psychoanalytic questions can be summarized
by the slogan of conservatism." He agreed that the "applica-

tion of psychoanalysis to sociology is the main task" and the "first applications of this kind à la Reik or Róheim have been basically wrong." However, he wrote to Kardiner, "the opposite danger does also exist today . . . one might neglect or underestimate the specific discoveries of Freud and the unconscious" (LX/11 August 1939/9).

As was his habit, Fenichel reviewed the book at length and sent the review with a letter to Kardiner. He sympathized with the book's social orientation but not with its rejection of instinct theory. He told Kardiner, "the libido theory has never denied that the personal structures are formed by the frustrating and limiting influences of the outer world" (LXVIII/July 1940/6). Kardiner expressed "deep chagrin" at Fenichel's criticism and failure "to grasp what I was driving at" (LXX/10 August 1940/7). Kardiner subsequently joined Sandor Rado in breaking away from the New York Institute to establish a separate clinic associated with Columbia University.

The same theoretical and tactical jockeying marked Fenichel's relations with Karen Horney, Margaret Mead, and, above all, Erich Fromm. Fenichel saluted Horney's attack on "extreme biologism," which, he noted, remained a constitutional failing of current psychoanalysis. Yet Fenichel anticipated that Horney's receptivity to the "social moment" would entail a "turning away from Freud and a surrendering of specific analytic knowledge" (?XXXIX/11 September 1937/7).

Horney's *Neurotic Personality of Our Time* fully confirmed Fenichel's fears. While it hinted of socialism, her book completely neglected sexuality; ultimately, Fenichel concluded in a review, it can explain neither the social nor psychic structures (XL/23 October 1937/11). He sent the review to Horney who judged it "very fair," but reiterated that they fundamentally differed on instinct theory: "I see it as something which must be overcome" (XLII/7 January 1938/9).

With Fromm, Fenichel maintained the broadest discussions. In Germany they had moved in the same left-wing analytic circles. For several years Fromm belonged to the Institute of Social Research (or, the Frankfurt School), which included Max Horkheimer, T. W. Adorno, and Herbert Marcuse. In the Frankfurt School's journal, Fromm published an article on the social bases of psychoanalytic therapy which prompted Fenichel to reestablish the contact with Fromm that exile had severed. Fromm's essay attacked Freud's therapeutic posture—noninvolvement—as a liberalism camouflaging a cold authoritarianism; Fromm praised Ferenczi as the more radical analyst who dared to encourage love and warmth in therapy. Freud remained a nineteenth-century aristocratic liberal, according to Fromm, correct in his therapeutic behavior, but fundamentally unable to affirm the happiness of his patients.[9]

Fenichel commented in the *Rundbriefe* that on many points Fromm's critique recalled Reich's, although Fromm did not cite Reich. Fenichel wrote to Fromm, suggesting they resume their "interrupted connection": those devoted to a "social psychoanalysis" should work together. Yet he rejected much of Fromm's essay. Fromm's point that Freud was a child of his time was undoubtedly correct. "How could it be otherwise?" To polemicize against Freud as a repressive bourgeois missed the mark. It reminded Fenichel of Reich "who always reproached Freud for not being a Communist" (XXIII/3 March 1936/12).

Fenichel also did not accept Fromm's critique of Freud's therapeutic practice, a recurring objection lodged against Freud by the neo-Freudians. Many neo-Freudians championed Ferenczi; by encouraging affection and love in therapy, he broke with Freud's asceticism. Fenichel defended Freud's orthodoxy as more radical than Ferenczi's reform. The neutrality prescribed by orthodox psychoanalysis, he wrote to Fromm, does not deny the patient's claim to happiness. Nor did he agree that Ferenczi's teachings on love radically transcended the social taboos that beset Freud. In fact, in his last years a reactionary flavor permeated Ferenczi's ideas. Alluding to Ferenczi's final illness and mental deterioration, which his followers have always contested, Fenichel wrote that he did not know why Fromm celebrated "the great Ferenczi in this period of his decline." To be sure he retained his "genial flashes of insight"; but this did not suffice to elevate him to a "revolutionary analyst who overcame liberalism" (XXIII/3 March 1936/12).

Fromm responded in detail to Fenichel's comments. Ferenczi was no revolutionary, yet his relationship with patients struck a different note from Freud's. Fromm also explained his dearth of references to Reich "on personal as well as factual" grounds. Personally he found intolerable Reich's "pathological self-love and arrogance." Moreover, despite appearances, he and Reich tap antagonistic traditions. "Philosophically Reich in no way represents historical materialism; rather he represents a mechanical materialism. . . . In reality he has never understood Marxism." While unyielding about Ferenczi, Fenichel completely accepted Fromm's evaluation of Reich. Reich's "impossible behavior," he noted, compelled his own move from "secure Oslo to insecure Prague." In general, Fenichel believed, Reich has rendered more difficult the project of a social psychoanalysis (XXV/23 April 1936/10).

Even as Fenichel endeavored to reestablish relations, Fromm was moving in a neo-Freudian direction. After Fromm published several essays clearly influenced by Horney and other neo-Freudians, Fenichel asked, "What became of Fromm's Marxism?" (90/10 July 1942/14) When Fromm's *Escape from Freedom* appeared, a transition work marking his departure from classical psychoanalysis, Fenichel published a long critical review. "For the purpose of avoiding and correcting mistakes which psychoanalysis admittedly has made," he charged that Fromm, Kardiner, Horney, and others "abandon psychoanalysis altogether instead of applying it in a better way."[10] Fromm embraced a vague social idealism which he falsely imagined was more "real" and "concrete" than Freud's antiquated concepts.

Privately, however, Fenichel sounded another note: the theoretical issues could not be cleaved from the plight of their circle. To the version of the Fromm review he circulated in the *Rundbriefe* Fenichel added that it was "regretable" that "we" do not write better books than the neo-Freudians. "Perhaps it could be made possible that such better books be written by the reestablishment of our old and forgotten habit of discussing important issues of Marxist psychoanalysis among ourselves" (86/3 March 1942/1). He increasingly accompanied his criticisms of the neo-Freudians with the same lament. "We," the more political and radical analysts, have surrendered to the neo-Freudians.

In 1937 he sharply criticized Margaret Mead's *Sex and Temperament* for its "unsurpassable naïveté, bourgeois prejudice, and sociological ignorance" (XXXIII/1 February 1937/9). Eight years later when he evaluated another book by Mead, *And Keep Your Powder Dry*, regret mollified his critique. Fenichel, troubled by his group's minimal productivity and visibility, concluded that Mead's book was idealistic and inadequate, yet "its task is our task," the concrete investigation of social and character structures. In one of his final letters, he noted that fifteen years ago this was "our" program; but we have watched as non-psychoanalytic thinkers assumed the lead. "When will we have the opportunity to sit down together? . . . We all have ideas which go far beyond what Margaret Mead says." Today, he commented, the analysts know neither anthropology nor history; and if a few anthropologists command psychoanalysis they are deficient in history and sociology (114/2 January 1945/13).

# Freudians Against Freudians

The isolation of the Fenichel group was defined, perhaps caused, by their distance from both the neo-Freudians and the psychoanalytic conservatives. Even as Fenichel fired away at the neo-Freudians, he reiterated that the opposite extreme, a psychological reductionism which explained everything by the Oedipus complex, still flourished. Ernest Jones's "Evolution and Revolution"[11] reminded Fenichel of the vigor of this psychologism. "It is enlightening to see how the 'leaders' of 'orthodox' psychoanalysis have learned nothing in the last years" (87/22 March 1942/9). That the conservatives continued to prosper was brought home to Fenichel by a critical review of Kardiner by Róheim and a review of Fromm by Menninger; these reviews he considered "obviously unjust" (83/27 November 1941/9). Fenichel often reminded the others that "we" must not cease to distinguish ourselves from the reactionary critiques of the neo-Freudians.

This delicate theoretical posture suffered when translated into the protean world of organizational politics. When Horney and her followers broke with the New York Society, the Fenichel circle faced unpleasant choices: they could not support the revisionists, even though they applauded their general orientation; and they also harbored serious differences with the conservatives who maintained the organization. This "paradoxical situation" pained Fenichel. The Horney group challenged the official organization partly because it failed properly to assess social factors; but Fenichel entertained "no doubt" that we must be against the Horney group since they renounced the essence of psychoanalysis (80/3 September 1941/1).

In the middle of World War II the symmetry between the military and psychoanalytic battle seemed obvious to Fenichel. The alliance of the reactionary Western forces and revolutionary Soviet forces mirrored the configuration within psychoanalysis. An ironic coalition of conservatives and revolutionaries composed the Allies. There is an analogy . . . in our little field of psychoanalytic politics. . . . In spite of some correct criticisms which are brought forward by the "advanced" people [Horney's splinter group, the Association for the Advancement of Psychoanalysis], there is no doubt that they are going to abandon psychoanalysis and Freud altogether. . . . We are forced to side in this matter unreservedly with the "conservative forces" (89/15 May 1942/1).

The *Rundbriefe* never consumed all of Fenichel's enormous writing energies. In Prague, his home after the break with Reich, he completed a number of penetrating essays. He also gave a course of lectures in Vienna, *Problems of Psychoanalytic Technique*, which has recently been called a "neglected classic" in its field.[12] Several of the sociological essays from this period belong to the best of his oeuvre. Perhaps because he had by then parted from Reich, the essays were not burdened with leaden discussions on the parallels between Marxism and psychoanalysis; these preoccupations had disfigured the piece he had published earlier in Reich's journal.[13] And unlike the following years in the United States, the political psychoanalytic community retained an identity that could still sustain—intellectually and emotionally—dissident theorizing.

"The Drive to Amass Wealth," a critique of Edward Glover, a discussion of Erich Fromm, an evaluation of Freud's theory of the death instinct, an essay on anti-Semitism, and other manuscripts were all products of these three years (1935–38). Since several of these works are included in Fenichel's *Collected Papers* they do not require lengthy description here. The essays on wealth and the death instinct partake of earlier discussions.

In 1932 Reich criticized Freud's new formulations of the death instinct as marking a theoretical retreat.[14] Fenichel generally seconded Reich's objections: the new theory of primary masochism and self-destruction shifted the cause of suffering from external repression to internal biological need, thus obviating a "critique of the social order."[15] As Fenichel put it, in accord with the theory of the death instinct, neurosis originates in a conflict of two kinds of instinctual energies, self-destructive and erotic. "Such an interpretation would mean a total elimination of the social factor from the etiology of neuroses, and would amount to a complete biologization of neuroses."[16]

In contrast to conventional studies, Fenichel's "Drive to Amass Wealth" is distinguished by its avoidance of antipsychoanalytic sociology or a psychoanalytic reductionism.[17] For Fenichel reductionism marred Ferenczi's contributions. Ferenczi passed too quickly from the child's interest in feces to the role of money; he ignored the decisive social institutions, as if capitalism itself arose out of the instincts to collect and accumulate.[18] To Fenichel, capitalism makes use of instincts but is not a product of them. "In the tendency to trace social institutions directly back to biological instincts, we see the same danger of *biologizing,*" which deemphasizes "actual infantile experiences." "If any individual wishes to collect things, money does not result therefrom." However, a superficial sociology is equally unsatisfactory: the proposition of economic primacy is "correct," but too general and abstract.[19]

Fenichel's "Psychoanalysis of Anti-Semitism," originally delivered before a Prague Zionist group, was published in several versions; the last was included in *Anti-Semitism: A Social Disease,* edited by Ernst Simmel.[20] This essay may be the best Fenichel wrote; incisive and original it suggests Fenichel's brilliance once he relinquished the usual systematization. It ranged beyond the usual theories of anti-Semitism to meditate on the problem of the Jew as the archaic and uncanny—the unconscious—which must be eradicated.

To be sure, Fenichel emphasized the limits of a narrow psychoanalytic approach to anti-Semitism. "The instinctual structure of the average man in Germany was no different in

1935 from what it was in 1925." Consequently psychoanalysis alone cannot explain the success of nazism. In the six years that separated the two published versions of his essay, Fenichel diluted his Marxism. The later version concludes by reminding the reader of the importance of the prevailing social and economic circumstances, which are "beyond the scope of this paper. However, this does not mean that they are of secondary importance."[21] The earlier version, by contrast, states that anti-Semitism is a "weapon in the class warfare dominating the present civilized world."[22]

Four other articles from these years not included in the *Collected Papers* should also be mentioned here. The first, a series of questions about Engels's *The Peasant War in Germany*, was evidently written for a study group.[23] The second evaluated Fromm's lengthy contribution to the Frankfurt School tome, *Authorität und Familie*, in which Fromm developed the concept of the authoritarian-masochistic character.[24] While chiding Fromm for an overdescriptive approach, Fenichel praised the essay.[25]

Edward Glover's *War, Sadism, and Pacificism* (1933) was the subject of the third piece. Fenichel found nothing to recommend in Glover's reductionist discussion of war. Real social interests and economic forces do not enter Glover's account. "Glover's main error can be formulated this way: all psychological factors that partake of war, he treats as causes of war."[26] Glover wrote an unfriendly reply, deriding Fenichel's review as the usual fare of socialists or Communists; he noted that Freud was in full agreement with his book and that psychoanalysis was incompatible with all "isms." Fenichel counterreplied: if my honored teacher agrees with you, then here I "cannot follow" Professor Freud.[27]

The fourth manuscript is a lecture Fenichel delivered to a cultural society in Basel, "Psychoanalyse und Gesellschaftswissenschaften" ("Psychoanalysis and the Social Sciences"). Making no claims for originality, Fenichel argued that neither psychoanalysis nor Marxism could be ignored. "Psychologism" failed to do justice to the great social realities of war and capitalism. While a distrust of much psychology is justified, especially academic psychology, it is impossible to comprehend social dependency and authoritarianism without psychoanalysis. The emotional life can only be studied with psychoanalysis, which is not a universal science but an aid in social theorizing.[28]

Fenichel had lectured in Basel when he toured Europe in early 1938, a dark year for central Europe. The Austrian Anschluss was eight weeks off; the Munich Pact and dismemberment of Czechoslovakia were on the horizon. In addition to Switzerland, Fenichel lectured in France, the Netherlands, and England. He was not reassured; the prospects for life and work looked bleak in Europe. He concluded that a "reduced security of existence" threatened everyone. He had never viewed his stay in Prague as more than "temporary."[29] Even prior to his trip through Europe, he had decided to emigrate to the United States; now he redoubled his efforts to obtain the necessary visas and permits.

Fenichel's few years in Prague left a deep imprint on Czechoslovakian psychoanalysis, which was then in its formative phase.[30] He commanded a small group of closely knit analysts. The other senior analysts were friends from Vienna and Berlin —Annie Reich, Steff Bornstein, and Henry Lowenfeld. With his inexhaustable energy Fenichel set out organizing the informal Prague analytic community into a regular branch of the International Society.

Later, in Los Angeles, Fenichel fondly recalled the intensity and warmth of the Prague analytic atmosphere. It did not last: Europe was becoming a Nazi colony. A 1938 report from the Prague analysts dryly noted that "the events in central Europe" have brought an end to the Vienna Society and with it the associated Prague group. It observed that half the membership had already left Prague in 1938; the other half intended to follow in 1939.[31] In fact by 1939, of the senior analysts, only Steff Bornstein remained, and she died that same year. Dr. Brief and Therese Bondy, who were associated with the Prague group, were killed in concentration camps. A single analyst, Theodor Dusužkov, survived the German occupation.[32]

To obtain the requisite guarantees of support and employment, Fenichel entered into negotiations with the Psychoanalytic Study Group of Los Angeles; its president, Ernst Simmel, had arrived in California in 1934. Simmel had already enabled Frances Deri, a close acquaintance from Berlin, to settle in Los Angeles. Negotiations with Fenichel resulted in a contract in which Fenichel agreed to teach half-time for three years "the science of psychoanalysis to the members of the Study Group." Seven members of the Study Group, which included several professors of theoretical physics, agreed to contribute in order to pay Fenichel 250 dollars a month.[33]

In the early spring of 1938 Fenichel delivered a parting address to the increasingly nervous Prague analysts. He surveyed the grim scene. The Nazis had just entered Vienna; everywhere Freud's works were proscribed. He observed that the fate of psychoanalysis no longer depended on whether the analytic community successfully opposed this or that deviation. "The inner developments of the so-called 'analytic movement' lose their importance. The fate of psychoanalysis depends on the fate of the world and science in general" (XLVIII/25 June 1938/19). Nor did he agree with those who decided that, in the fight against Fascist extremism, they should become extreme leftists.

He told the Prague group he once believed that the authentic task of psychoanalysis was its elaboration into a theory of human culture and society; however, he concluded that those tasks, and hopes, belonged to the distant past. In the Fascist lands "Geist" is being murdered, lies spread, and every effort is made to make "people dumb instead of intelligent." Faced with barbarism we must become "very modest." We can count on no great discoveries or breakthroughs; the single task is to preserve psychoanalysis—to hold out. Perhaps barbarism will spread, and psychoanalysis along with all culture will disappear. Nevertheless we must work to preserve psychoanalysis. "The issue is not to heal this or that neurotic, but of applying thought generally to the events of psychic life . . . a living thought which is orientated towards the fullness of reality" (XLVIII/25 June 1938/19).

For Fenichel, this single imperative—the preservation of classical psychoanalysis—required abandoning Europe.

When Alexander wrote not long ago "Born and educated in America" he was sure that science had no more future in a Europe torn asunder; and that one must give up the European connection, and embrace glorious America. We, who knew how recent his Americanism was, laughed heartily. But isn't he right?

Fenichel closed his address with remarks adapted from a poem he had written, "Dennoch" ("Nevertheless").

Today the prospects for living thought are poor. Reason is challenged by war, and has turned gloomy. Many are oppressed; many are in need; and whoever thinks is threatened. Raw stupidity mixes with reason. . . . What once was is past. However, authentic integrity does not know defeat. When pressed, it hardens, and stands stronger: it can wait. Where there is still truth, it will be preserved, even if it must flee far. Sadly, only in America do we find hope. (XLVIII/25 June 1938/19)

Several days after this address, with his wife and child, Fenichel left Prague. The family flew to France and at Le Havre they boarded the S.S. *Manhattan*—"The Largest Steamer Ever Built in America"—which was packed with central European Jews streaming toward the United States.

# CHAPTER SIX

# The Illusion of a Future: Political Psychoanalysis in the United States

AS SOON as Fenichel arrived in the United States, he began meeting with old and new acquaintances in New York to discuss the situation of psychoanalysis. He traveled to New Haven and Boston and then proceeded by train to Los Angeles, stopping in Chicago, Topeka, and San Francisco to lecture and confer with other analysts. His first *Rundbrief* from America, a monster almost eighty pages long, detailed his findings; it was typically impersonal with only the vaguest clues to his responses to New York or to the expanse of the country, or to Los Angeles. Only his poetry allows a few glimpses of his private feelings. A poem, "Los Angeles Limited," written on the train crossing the continent, hinted of his weariness and of his fears of the California life that awaited him.

Like all immigrants, the newly arrived analysts were plagued by cultural shocks and misunderstandings. En route to Los Angeles, Fenichel stopped in Topeka, where Karl Menninger had established a psychoanalytic center and haven for foreign analysts. Fenichel found a world little resembling Prague or Berlin; he also imagined or sensed Menninger's hostility to his poor English and foreign eating habits.[1]

At Menninger's request, Fenichel prepared a lecture. Troubled by his imperfect pronunciation, Fenichel sought out other foreign analysts for aid; they were of little help. Martin Grotjahn, another refugee, recalled that Fenichel wanted to talk about something called "penis envoy." "That did not sound right," recounted Grotjahn, "and I tentatively suggested . . . 'penis ivy.' A suggestion by another immigrant 'envy' was rejected as too unlikely by Otto and me." Fenichel lectured "respected by all and understood by none. 'Penis envoy' finally brought down the house."[2]

In the United States Fenichel immediately associated with embattled Freudians—or so they viewed themselves—loyal to classical psychoanalysis. They agreed with Freud who passionately, almost obsessively, believed that American culture endangered his discoveries by subordinating them to a pragmatic psychiatry. That visits to North America seemed to precipitate major psychoanalytic defections—from Jung to Ferenczi—did not increase Freud's fondness for the United States. He once suggested to Max Eastman that he write a book on "the miscarriage of American civilization." "What makes you hate America so?" Eastman inquired. "Hate America?" he said, "I don't hate America, I regret it!"[3]

Fenichel did not shrink from identifying with the spirit and letter of European psychoanalysis; he little tolerated those who rushed to assimilate. A phrase from a letter by another recent immigrant, Sandor Rado, riled him. On behalf of the American Psychoanalytic Association, Rado had written to the international organization using the words "we Americans." For Fenichel, Rado exhibited unseemly haste in casting off his European garb.

Fascism compelled the political Freudians to retreat. As Fenichel put it in his parting lecture from Prague, the political Freudians must withdraw and preserve classical psychoanalysis; this was the best the times allowed. The situation in the United States reinforced this deployment of energies; conditions did not prompt political Freudians to advance a more social or militant psychoanalysis. The weakness of a credible Marxism; the relative newness of psychoanalysis; the geographic dispersion of the analysts; and the tenuous legal status of the immigrants all worked effectively against a political psychoanalysis. In addition, the medicalization proceeded most rapidly in the United States, undermining the cultural and political implications of psychoanalysis.

Fenichel's public writings reflected these realities; they barely breathed of his private and political sentiments. But a reader who read to the final pages of his straitlaced *Psychoanalytic Theory of Neurosis,* attuned to the cautious idiom, could pick up a number of clues. Fenichel espouses here a rigorous historical perspective. He writes:

Neuroses do not occur out of biological necessity, like aging. . . .
Neuroses are social diseases . . . the outcome of unfavorable and socially determined educational measures, corresponding to a given and historically developed social milieu. . . . They cannot be changed without corresponding change in the milieu.[4]

In the final pages of this text Fenichel reiterates several of his principles. Sharp limits beset the therapeutic possibilities of psychoanalysis. "Faced with the enormous neurotic (and non-neurotic) misery of today, we are sometimes near to despair, realizing that we can help only five to ten persons a year." There is "consolation," however, in the "general application" of psychoanalysis.

Not because primitive instincts are still effective within us do we have wars, misery and neuroses; rather, because we have not yet learned to avoid wars and misery by a more reasonable and less contradictory regulation of social relations, our instincts are still kept in an unfavorable form.[5]

After almost six hundred dense pages of categories and descriptions, these inelegant formulations effectively smothered the message of socialism, "a more reasonable and less contradictory regulation of social relations."

The *Rundbriefe* kept alive the torch of a political psychoanalysis, but even it flickered. More and more, talk of the organizational threats to classical psychoanalysis—the revamping of psychoanalytic institutes—displaced theoretical discussions of a social psychoanalysis. Nevertheless Fenichel continued to monitor events and evaluate literature germane to the group's original project.

His comments on Soviet Marxism indicate how far he had traveled from his earlier uncritical praise. When Vera Schmidt, the Russian analyst, died, he recalled his "first disappointment" with her. When he asked her about the relationship of Marxism and psychoanalysis, she had replied there was nothing to discuss, since there was only one correct form of Marxism "which the Soviet Union and its leader Stalin represented" (XLVIII/25 June 1938/2).

A pro-Soviet article that appeared in a psychology journal provoked some sharper reflections.[6] Fenichel remembered the essay, also a paean to the Soviet Union, that he himself had published fourteen years earlier on Bolschevo:

A short time after my article appeared we saw "The Road to Life," and we had discussion evenings about this picture in which we were already a little less enthusiastic. We used to criticize the lack of serious consideration of all sex problems, and used to hear from the Soviet Union the nonsensical reply: "Neurosis and sexual problems exist in capitalist societies. . . ." Now it seems nearly an atavism when fourteen years later, we again get the same thing to read with the same enthusiasm. (118/13 May 1945/5)

Though Fenichel renounced an uncritical adoration of the Soviet Union, he never renounced a political vision. In one of the darkest moments of the war he wrote a poem about the first of May ("Erster Mai"), the international day of labor. He wrote that barbarism and evil afflict the world; everything is empty; everything is burnt out. Yet, Marx perceives a way out, the goal embedded in the working class. "Whoever lives must try."

Fenichel tried. In Los Angeles he joined a vast community of German exiles who regularly discussed the prospects of war and world change. The community included such luminaries as Thomas Mann, Franz Werfel, and Bertolt Brecht among the hundreds, perhaps thousands, of others. Thomas Mann's wife Katia recalled "in California we saw more German writers than we had in Munich."[7]

These exiles also included Max Horkheimer, T. W. Adorno, and occasionally Leo Lowenthal, all key figures of the Frankfurt School. Drawing on Erich Fromm, the Frankfurt School had devoted itself to psychoanalysis as part of its larger neo-Marxist "critical theory." Ernst Simmel, a friend of Horkheimer's, probably served as a bridge between the adherents of "critical theory" and Fenichel's own political psychoanalysis. It was also Simmel who organized a conference on anti-Semitism at which Fenichel and Bernfeld as well as Adorno and Horkheimer gave papers. Both Adorno and Horkheimer joined the Los Angles Psychoanalytic Study Group, which was essentially run by Simmel and Fenichel. On the shores of the Pacific, an intense German culture was burning brightly.

Horkheimer and Lowenthal occasionally attended the seminar that Fenichel conducted. His Literature Seminar, open to analysts and nonanalysts, usually consisted of a lecture by a participant followed by a general discussion. The topics ranged far beyond technical analytic issues. For Fenichel, this seminar summoned up the study groups in Prague and Berlin. Lowenthal recalls its atmosphere: "I had the feeling that it was one of the last refuges of the avant-garde period of the psychoanalytic movement before it became a commercialized specialty."[8]

It was at this seminar that Lowenthal, when Horkheimer was ailing, delivered Horkheimer's lecture, "Individual in Mass Culture." Fenichel judged it "very stimulating" but objected to some of Horkheimer's formulations. He maintained that Horkheimer minimized the capitalist nature of mass culture by viewing it as a necessary by-product of advanced industry (88/12 April 1942/2). This objection reflects Fenichel's lingering attachment to a more rigorous or conventional Marxism than prevailed among the Frankfurt School; he feared that the Marxist critique of capitalism might be diluted into a vague critique of technology and machinery—his objection to Fromm's work. Fromm imagined that the "helplessness" and "powerlessness" of individuals derived from machinery itself, not from its capitalist use. "Not the immensity of the machine matters," Fenichel stated like a good Marxist, "but its use by monopolistic capitalism."[9]

After another lecture by Horkheimer, "The End of Reason," and after perusing the Frankfurt School journal, Fenichel concluded that the Frankfurt School shared Fromm's theoretical flaws. He considered "The End of Reason," "very interesting and significant" but too vague about the material base of mass culture (91/11 August 1942/8). The printed version of the lecture provided more proof of Horkheimer's "undialecti-cal" approach; he thinks, Fenichel wrote, "machinery is an evil."[10] Fenichel agreed that the "apparatus" devours any op-position; however, the apparatus is in itself neutral; what mat-ters is how it is used. He concluded: "One really often gets the impression that Marx today is handled by the 'Marxists' in a very similar way as Freud is handled by the 'Freudians'" (91/11 August 1942/9).

Fenichel's meditations on Marxism and its discontents ra-pidly diminished; they were clearly subordinated to his primary task, the preservation of classical analysis. He did observe, and saluted, a greater receptivity to social theory in the United States than in Europe; even the physicists he encountered were open to social issues. In 1939 he attended a seminar at the California Institute of Technology, where psychoanalysis and sociology were discussed. Fenichel was very impressed by the interest of the scientists in a sociological psychoanalysis.

One participant, identified by Fenichel as "a Marxist physics professor from Berkeley" was J. Robert Oppenheimer, who shortly afterward headed the Los Alamos research team that developed the atomic bomb. (Still later Oppenheimer's "secu-rity clearance" was lifted, partly because of his earlier left-wing connections.) Now he seemed concerned with psychoanalysis and Marxism. According to Fenichel, following the seminar, he sent Oppenheimer a copy of his (German) essay, "Psycho-analysis as the Nucleus of a Future Dialectical-Materialistic Psychology." This originally appeared in Reich's journal and boasts some of Fenichel's most wooden Marxism. The essay charmed Oppenheimer: "I was delighted with it," he wrote Fenichel, "with the many thoughtful and incisive points, but above all with the evident and rare sincerity of your apprecia-tion of both analysis and Marxism." He even offered to translate the essay, suggesting that Fenichel submit it to a Marxist journal. Fenichel demurred (?LIX/15 July 1939/17).

Yet Fenichel recorded few victories among professional analysts; instead he witnessed everywhere a flight from classical analysis. After reading a summary of a psychoanalytic congress, he observed that no one talked of sexuality, proof of the self-sublimation of analysis. "How right Reich was once again!" Fenichel noted, alluding to Reich's belief that establishment psychoanalysis deemphasized sexuality. In England the followers of Melanie Klein steadily increased their influence; while in America the medical doctors and neo-Freudians threatened to tame psychoanalysis. He saw the Americans streamlining psychoanalysis so as to fit it neatly into their offices; they stripped it of its cultural and political implications. In fact the Americans preferred pure clinical practice to any theorizing. Fenichel recounted an exchange that symbolizes the American attitude. "One colleague said in a debate . . . 'We have to above all teach what we understand and not theories.' Upon which I replied: 'Many of us understand theory' " (XLVIII/25 June 1938/3).

To be sure Fenichel considered "Americans" to include immigrants such as Rado who enthusiastically identified with their new homeland. Fenichel had no love for Rado, whom he called "the dictator" of the New York analytic scene. According to Fenichel, Rado championed pure practice and a pragmatic vocabulary against what he called the useless theorizing of a baroque psychoanalysis. Fenichel summarized the sentiment of the New York group: "We are practitioners and no longer want endless theoretical discussions!" If "practice" meant an improved grasp of reality and impatience with vapid theorizing, Fenichel concurred.

But no; when one speaks of praxis in New York, it does not mean "an orientation towards reality." Quick therapies are demanded, and all psychology that might disrupt this goal is dubbed "theory." Rado says one can either pursue the aim of healing people or of enjoying clever thoughts *(geistreichen Gedanken)*. It does not occur to Rado that with the help of intelligent thinking, people could be better and more radically healed; that their actions could be anticipated and influenced; that theory is orientated towards practice; and that a praxis that has no theory is worthless. (XLVIII/25 June 1938/3)

The personal situation of the analysts aggravated the theoretical disarray. The New York analytic community first struck Fenichel as a lion's den, where "each was against each." A situation of pure competition reigned. A libidinal commitment to a common cause no longer existed; even a sentimental link to Freud had disappeared, since he was personally known to few of them. Each connived and conspired as if every other analyst were stealing patients; yet there was no shortage of patients. A distrust of the refugee permeated the community or, at least, Fenichel sensed a distrust. For this reason he did not want to surface openly with his allies as an oppositional group dedicated to preserving classical analysis. They were all foreigners, and their appearance as an organized circle would only feed suspicions.

This tactic was frequently debated by his circle in the *Rundbriefe*, but Fenichel did not waver; a public group would be a mistake. "We have too little power, and consequently the mood of opposition to the immigrants, which already exists, would increase," exacerbating the antagonisms between the American and foreign analysts (LIV/6 February 1939/4). Fenichel did look for openings; he reported in deepest confidence that Hans Sachs was beginning a new magazine, *American Imago*, and that the magazine had been secretly charged by Freud to rally the classical, and now embattled, analysts.

The fight to preserve classical analysis was fought with letters, proposals, and organizational amendments. Any visions of a cultural and political psychoanalysis contracted to meetings and minutes. This was not the stuff to quicken the soul, but Fenichel jumped in with his usual energy. The practical questions of the regulation of psychoanalytic societies and institutes preoccupied Fenichel and many other analysts; these were the questions of the day.

The Psychoanalytic Study Group of Los Angeles was itself a source of conflict. Organized in 1935 with Simmel as its president, it never sought or received official recognition from the American Psychoanalytic Association (although many of its members were affiliated with other official chapters).[11] At an anniversary celebration Simmel declared that the study group was proposing to rescue psychoanalysis from a mechanization that threatened it.[12] Fenichel, who often praised his Los Angeles seminar, had no illusions about California as a psychoanalytic oasis. "I too am often longing for the discussions we used to have in Europe" (98/7 May 1943/10).

The policies and informality of analysts in Los Angeles were unavoidably affected by the larger problems of reorganization of the national association, the American Psychoanalytic Association. Eventually the West Coast analysts would have to affiliate with the restructured national organization. Along with analysts across the country they debated organizational proposals—for instance, the definitions of full, associated, and guest membership in the association. Because of the influx of foreign analysts and a growing interest among Americans, issues which the Europeans had already argued, and sometimes settled, now had to be reopened: these included questions of the general organization of the national association, the establishment of training institutes, and the status of lay analysts.[13]

In each dispute, Fenichel sided with the "conservatives," those he considered loyal to the spirit of Freud. However, on the question of lay analysis, his fidelity to Freud entailed disloyalty to most conservatives, who generally opposed nonmedical psychoanalysts. Fenichel's orthodox unorthodoxy did not prove very successful; he was soundly defeated on almost every issue.

He was unable to deter efforts to detach the American association from the binding regulations of the international association. When Fenichel arrived in 1938 these efforts had reached their peak. Since the center of psychoanalysis had shifted to the United States, the American analysts no longer wanted to subordinate themselves to the international organization, which they considered distant and indifferent to the specific American situation. In 1938, the American association declared its effective independence from the international one. To Fenichel the weakening of organizational ties encouraged the fragmentation of psychoanalytic theory.

The question of institutes often occupied Fenichel. Political parties are to Marxists what psychoanalytic institutes are to psychoanalysts. Institutes are where analysts are trained; and only certain analysts are certified to be "training" analysts. Due to the nature of the analytic experience, the candidates often become partisans of their teachers' (and analysts') doctrines. Hence for all those concerned with professional psychoanalysis, the nature of the institutes was a critical question: How were they established? Who was certified to teach? What was to be taught?

The issue of teaching and training precipitated the first important split in the American Psychoanalytic Association; the Karen Horney group exited claiming that they were being denied a role in teaching and training.[14] At the same time the American association considered proposals to permit any group of qualified analysts to establish training institutes, thus allowing multiple institutes in the same city. For Fenichel the proposals directly threatened the integrity of psychoanalysis; they encouraged analysts to promote their own particular theoretical versions of psychoanalysis.[15] Indeed the proposals, which eventually passed, initiated a period of new institutes.

The issue of lay analysis touched Fenichel most profoundly. Here he was completely loyal to Freud. The future of psychoanalysis as more than a medical treatment, as a larger theory, depended on lay analysts. For Fenichel, though not for Freud, this larger theory implied a critical political vision; both nevertheless perceived that monopolization by medical doctors risked degrading psychoanalysis into a technique with no cultural or political consequences.

Freud's support of lay analysis was unpopular everywhere, but especially in the United States. Very few doctors defended nonmedical practitioners. As the American association reorganized, it debated the status of lay analysis. By 1938 the discussion was over: the American association would not certify new lay analysts. Yet sensitive areas remained unresolved, and hotly disputed, for instance, the status of lay analysts who had already been practicing.

The issue was particularly delicate in California since many lay analysts had settled on the West Coast. Included in this category were not only nonmedical analysts such as Siegfried Bernfeld, but also analysts such as Simmel and Fenichel, who had European medical degrees which were not honored in the United States. Legally they were lay analysts. The conditions under which the California groups could join the American association were the subject of endless negotiations. Neither Simmel nor Fenichel wanted to join a psychoanalytic association in which lay analysts were second-class citizens. The issue haunted the Los Angeles society even after the deaths of Fenichel and Simmel. The preponderance of lay analysts in the Los Angeles Society prompted one group in 1950 to split off from that organization. To underscore its medical orientation the new group called itself the Society for Psychoanalytic Medicine of Southern California.[16] (This society later dropped "Medicine" from its name to become the Southern California Psychoanalytic Institute and Society.)

The issue of lay analysis and his own status in the psychoanalytic community weighed heavily on Fenichel. With distress he charted the "progressive suppression of nonphysician analysts" and "the progressive degradation of psychoanalysis into a psychiatric method." He was unwilling to compromise on an issue vital to the health of psychoanalysis; it is essential, he stated, to avoid "any Munich," that is, a compromise on lay analysis that would gain nothing but additional setbacks (90/10 July 1942/5).

His own credentials as a practicing analyst were not in question. To be sure, like other foreign-licensed medical doctors, he existed in a legal no-man's-land; yet the likelihood of his being blocked from the practice or teaching of psychoanalysis was slight. Nevertheless, Fenichel believed that his theoretical, and perhaps personal, position could be undermined if he legally remained a lay analyst; he would always be vulnerable. He did not want to fight for lay analysis as a lay analyst; and in order to defend unpopular theoretical perspectives he wanted to be personally unassailable. As he wrote to a friend, he decided to deprive his political and theoretical adversaries of "the cheap argument 'and he is not even an American M.D.' "[17]

It is difficult to grasp fully the feelings that in 1945 drove Fenichel at the age of forty-seven to obtain an American medical degree. Requirements for immigrant doctors to receive official licensing differed from state to state. California required a one-year full-time resident internship. This entailed practicing medicine in hospital wards on a rotating schedule, usually without relief for thirty-six to forty-eight hours at a stretch.

For a man of almost fifty, these were not steps to be taken lightly; simply the physical strain of internship tired even young doctors. Moreover, Fenichel had not studied medicine for a quarter of a century—an additional burden. At the very least he would be thrown into an alien hospital environment with young American medical interns as colleagues. Finally, it would also necessitate the termination of Fenichel's psychoanalytic practice.

After Fenichel received his citizenship—a prerequisite for obtaining an American M.D. degree—he arranged to take an internship at a Los Angeles hospital. Before assuming his new role, he planned a trip to New York to visit friends; he also had to wind up his psychoanalytic practice. In the spring of 1945 he completed checking the galleys of his *Psychoanalytic Theory of Neurosis* and departed for New York.

On his return from New York, he sent out his last *Rundbrief*. For years, almost from the beginning, he had pondered the justification for his group. He was continually bothered by the less-than-full commitment of the others. He noted that he bore all the expenses and labor of the letters. At various times he had broached the question of whether they should continue, the last occasion being in 1941. The recipients responded by affirming the importance of the *Rundbriefe*. "The *Rundbriefe* are a form of organization, if a small one," a member of the circle stated. Fenichel was only half convinced. There can be no doubt that all "those interested in Marxist analysis should maintain a strong contact." However he questioned whether the "*Rundbriefe* in their current form are the right means to maintain such contact," and whether their organization was more fiction than fact (LXXIII/23 January 1941/1).

When Fenichel sent out his one hundredth letter, he indicated that it called for a celebration. "However, I do not feel like 'celebrating' on this occasion at all." He did not quite believe that the *Rundbriefe* were worth the effort (100/10 July 1943/1). Indeed the rate of distribution and the length of the *Rundbriefe* had gradually diminished. His trip to New York and his upcoming internship convinced him that the *Rundbriefe* belonged to the past. On 14 July 1945 Fenichel sent out his briefest letter, number 119; it was a single page.

The last letter began abruptly: "This is going to be the last *Rundbrief.*" He explained that his recent doubts as to the significance of the letters had not been allayed. He restated his conviction that for the moment the "fight" was not for a social psychoanalysis, but for "the very existence of Freudian psychoanalysis." He envisioned future splits in psychoanalysis in which their own "fraction" would play a role. "Sooner or later a kind of *Rundbriefe* will come into being in various places which will be very different from ours." Now, however, he had other tasks. In New York, he visited several recipients of the *Rundbriefe.* "I wondered whether somebody would suggest a meeting of our 'fraction.' Silently I thought that such a wish would be a sign that the *Rundbriefe* still have some meaning . . . . No one suggested a meeting." For Fenichel it was over.

He sent out his final *Rundbrief* and prepared for a new life. In the middle of the summer of 1945 Fenichel assumed his internship at the Cedars of Lebanon Hospital; he never finished it. In six months he was dead. The cause was attributed to a ruptured cerebral aneurysm. If the aneurysm was congenital, immediate circumstances may have been decisive in ending his life. He was working rotating night shifts as an intern. He complained frequently of fatigue; and he hoped to transfer to a hospital where night duty was not required. He was also overweight, and very much unlike himself, he expressed doubts about his command of medical knowledge. A visitor recalled him somewhat tragically: an older German-Jewish intellectual in a tight, ill-fitting white uniform. He died 22 January 1946; he had recently turned forty-eight.

Fenichel's colleague and friend, Ernst Simmel, died the following year. Max Horkheimer spoke of both of them at a memorial meeting.

It is this surrender to expediency which makes it so necessary to stress the philosophical content and origin of Freudianism, and few among the second generation of analysts were so keenly aware of it as the late Otto Fenichel and Ernst Simmel. These thinkers were opposed to the employee-mentality which tries to make everything "function" for the sake of machinery. . . . They resisted the trend of psychoanalysis being sold out by quick technicians within its own field. Science indeed was to replace metaphysics but science as a philosophical force. It should do away with metaphysical illusions such as prejudices and superstitions but should carry over the basic concepts of rationality: truth, freedom, and justice.[18]

# CHAPTER SEVEN

# The Americanization
# of Psychoanalysis

FENICHEL's death and the termination of the *Rundbriefe* closed a chapter in the history of psychoanalysis. Without a network of support, the members of the circle went their separate ways. They pursued their psychoanalytic practices and/or their writings, but their political commitments receded even further. George Gero and Edith Gyömröi wrote very little. A few essays by Barbara Lantos delved into the nature of work; their Marxist slant appealed to Herbert Marcuse, who cited them in his *Eros and Civilization.* [1] The more extended writings of Edith Jacobson and Annie Reich betrayed no particular politics, and Kate Friedländer died in 1949.

Wilhelm Reich remained public and productive and attracted devoted disciples; yet his work veered toward mystical science. In any event, as if to mark the end of a tradition to which he remained irrevocably linked, by the late 1940s, the United States government actively harassed Reich. This resulted in a federal complaint against his "orgone energy ac-

# The Americanization of Psychoanalysis

cumulator," a trial, and his imprisonment. In 1956 many of Reich's publications, including *The Mass Psychology of Fascism*, were incinerated in a New York city dump by the United States government. An American Civil Liberties Union press release "protesting the burning of Reich's publications was not picked up by any major newspaper in the United States."[2]

It does not seem entirely fortuitous that a Frankfurt School theorist—Max Horkheimer—recalled the critical spirit that pervaded the oeuvre of Fenichel and Simmel; for, in the decades after their deaths, the Frankfurt School kept alive a psychoanalysis still loyal to social theory. As the political Freudians dissipated, the Frankfurt School managed to gain a public identity as theorists defending Freud against the Freudians. Their relations with psychoanalysis reached back to Germany, where they had helped found the Frankfurt Psychoanalytic Institute[3] and it extended forward to books such as the *Authoritarian Personality* by T. W. Adorno and others, and *Eros and Civilization* by Marcuse.

Nevertheless the Frankfurt School remained very much outside the realm of American social sciences, and certainly of American psychoanalysis. Indeed, their own inability to make contact with American culture prompted Adorno and Horkheimer to return to Germany after the war. Marcuse stayed but, as even the subtitle to *Eros and Civilization*, "A Philosophical Inquiry into Freud," indicates, his work did not intersect with professional psychoanalysis. To be sure, apart from the Frankfurt School, others sought to revitalize psychoanalysis, but even the boldest efforts—for example, Norman O. Brown's *Life Against Death* (1959)—did not disturb its theoretical sleep.

Of course broad generalizations about the state of psychoanalysis, or any discipline, are suspect. Next to every pronouncement of decline and crisis may be found congratulations and self-congratulations of recent advances. Often judgments vary with the situation of the judge. Disgruntled outsiders register decay while prosperous insiders celebrate progress.

In recent years, a stiff, perhaps bracing, antipsychoanalytic wind has blown through the culture. To many observers humanist, behavioral, and "anti-psychology" psychologies inflicted heavy damage on psychoanalysis. Other critics have written psychoanalysis off as a nineteenth-century biological and reactionary enterprise; they have denounced its protracted therapy as ineffectual and elitist. With its conceptual life flagging and its audience hostile, the day of psychoanalysis seemed over.

Yet psychoanalysis always secured enough students and patients to survive through the years. Its endurance may have paid off. The newer psychologies are often more suspect than the psychoanalysis that they have sought to dislodge. Lessons drawn from pigeons and encounter groups, the romanticization of mental illness, and quick therapies are themselves vulnerable to grave criticism. Nor have these antipsychoanalytic psychologies generated social or political theories of any substance; here psychoanalysis remains alone. Finally the antipsychoanalytic wind has weakened, and a renewal of interest in psychoanalysis can be registered in diverse fields.

From the bleak, and obviously false, forecast of the demise of psychoanalysis, it is tempting to jump to the opposite extreme of anticipating a triumphant future. The revised outlook records a revival of attention and interest in psychoanalysis. Indeed, the eclipse of the political Freudians and their peculiar theorizing is proof not of regression but of progress. More precise categories have replaced speculative and outmoded approaches. Across the psychoanalytic field, researchers hone its conceptual edge. To its credit, this vision resists a rampant nostalgia, the inclination to glorify the early phases of psychoanalysis, or any science, as the heroic period.

Nevertheless if nostalgia is rife within the general culture,

# The Americanization of Psychoanalysis

within the sciences themselves a polar sentiment is much more frequent, the glorification of the latest discoveries. This theoretical narcissism is accompanied by a condescension toward earlier generations and their theories. That Freud and psychoanalysis were "nineteenth century" remains the breathtaking insight of twentieth-century pundits. New contributions bask in the self-satisfaction of advancing science.

The belief in automatic scientific progress must not be disparaged; it must be radically challenged. This requires seriously entertaining the opposite proposition, the possibility of regression and retreat. Here images of Dark Ages or tides of occultism mislead. Scientific regression in the modern period assumes the face of bright new facts and paradigms; neither by themselves constitute advances. Facts may accumulate while comprehension fades; theorists may polish their concepts while insight recedes. Is there progress from Hegel to Quine, Weber to Parsons, Freud to Skinner?

A recent book on Freud, *Freud, Biologist of the Mind*, exemplifies the scientific ethos of progress; it was written, appropriately, by a historian of science, Frank J. Sulloway, who just as appropriately subtitled his book "Beyond the Psychoanalytic Legend." Sulloway catalogs some twenty-six "myths" about Freud and psychoanalysis along with their twenty-six "functions." Sulloway punctures them all including myth #16, "that Freud discovered infantile sexuality and the unconscious," and myth #23, "that Freud's theories were given an inadequate, hostile and irrational reception." Sulloway instructs us that these "myths" serve only to legitimate psychoanalysis and the psychoanalytic movement. "This interlocking web of legend has been absolutely essential to the strategy of revolution employed by Freud and his loyal followers."[4]

Yet of the myths that animate the Western mind, few are older and more tenacious than the myth of the hero slaying myths. Sulloway's book fully conforms to this primal scientific myth; he bravely attacks the psychoanalytic "myths" that have deluded the world. In its allegiance to the scientific legend of progress, Sulloway's book may more aptly be turned on its head, the myth of the myth of Freud. Sulloway salves the scientific ethos insulted by the originality and speculations of Freud. Even his language—"interlocking web of legend" "strategy of revolution"—smacks of the intellectual cold warrior who annihilates his irrational opponent with unassailable facts. With a facile sociology of knowledge Sulloway leads us to the convocation of scientists where past thought is derided in the name of a better future.

The evolution of American psychoanalysis is reflected in its increasingly scientific vocabulary and theory. To be sure, Freud is often charged with saddling psychoanalysis with a scientific program and idiom; yet his American followers were more obsessed by the lure of scientific method. "Those critics who limit their studies to methodological investigations," Freud once remarked, "remind me of people who are always polishing their glasses instead of putting them on and seeing with them."[5]

The scientific psychoanalysis offered by Hartmann and Rapaport, as Joel Kovel has observed, derived less from conceptual imperatives than from "the need to develop psychoanalytic theory in this country with a view to its integration within prevailing normal science practice."[6] The price has been high: elaboration of structure and method has diminished depth and insight. The medical headquarters of psychoanalysis, moreover, has encouraged scientific classification in the service of clinical diagnoses.

The humanism and politics that medicalization squeezed out of psychoanalysis ultimately found a home in the universities. An account of current psychoanalysis cannot ignore the burst of academic psychoanalytic theorizing. In departments ranging from literature to history to sociology, psychoanalysis as a method or as a topic itself has attracted much attention. Nevertheless this activity expresses a crisis insofar as it is exterior to professional psychoanalysis; it is as if the best philosophy can be found in history departments or the best sociology in newspaper offices. Indeed this may be the case, but these dislocations generally indicate ossification in a discipline's natural habitat. A discipline takes to the road when its practitioners relinquish their original projects.

The flurry of psychoanalytic theorizing in the universities, however, is not as lively as it appears. From Harold Bloom to Jürgen Habermas, a second-generation Frankfurt School theorist, scholars deploy a brand of devitalized Freud. Especially in the literary field, where there is the most activity, unreadable self-promoting textual studies plump out the journals and books. Bloom writes: "In my reading of *Beyond [the Pleasure Principle]*'s chapter 5 as Freud's *Askesis,* his own sublimation, I implicitly questioned the coherence of the defense of sublimation even as I centered upon the hidden metaphor I name a contamination. I return to that metaphor of contamination for my conclusion."[7]

The stuff is designed to be listed in bibliographies and vitaes, not to be read. Its insularity offers an exact counterpart to medical psychoanalysis; both have exchanged Freud's openness and lucidity for a mangled jargon and vision. Freud's devotion to psychoanalysis as more than an arcane specialty extended to his devotion to accessible prose; he broached public issues— war or religion—in a public prose. Insofar as he was not exclusively a medical doctor or an academic specialist, he often wrote with simplicity on urgent public issues.

The corrosion of the prose of classical analysis is not a matter of shifting styles or shrinking talent; it reflects the fragmentation of a larger cultural universe into intellectual specialties and chain stores. Neither medical analysts nor psychoanalytic academics need or want to address a nonprofessional educated public; their reputations and careers are made within their departments or professions. This reality distorts the psychoanalytic prose and ultimately damages its spirit and substance.

As Bruno Bettelheim elegantly demonstrated, even Freud's own prose suffered from the imperatives of Anglo-American scientific life. The culture and humanism of Freud's German evaporated in the English translations that sought to validate psychoanalysis as a science. Translators regularly selected a scientific and mechanical vocabulary for Freud's more resonant, even poetic, German.

"Freud's direct and always deeply personal appeals to our common humanity," argues Bettelheim, "appear to readers of English as abstract, depersonalized, highly theoretical, erudite and mechanized—in short, 'scientific.' " For instance, a key word *Fehlleistung* ("faulty achievement") becomes a technical term "parapraxis." Even the fundamental *Ich* becomes translated almost everywhere as "ego" not "I," transforming it into a "jargon that no longer conveys the personal commitment we make when we say 'I' or 'me.' " Bettelheim, who has taught psychoanalysis for forty years to American psychiatrists, concludes:

Freud's ideas had to be transferred not only into a different language but into a different cultural environment—one in which most readers have only a nodding acquaintance with classical European literature. So most of Freud's allusions fall on deaf ears. Many of the expressions he used have been reduced to mere technical terms; the key words no longer have a multiplicity of special connotation, even though Freud chose them because they carried deep meaning and were vibrant with special humanist resonances.[8]

Nathan G. Hale, Jr., offered a more pedestrian example of linguistic Americanization. Freud had simply identified "love and work" *(Lieben und Arbeiten)* as the goal of life and successful therapy. Karl Menninger rendered this: "There are two fundamentals in life. One is the business of making love. The other is the business of making a living."[9]

The translation of psychoanalysis into a professional and scientific enterprise affected its language, spirit, breadth, and even those attracted to it; fewer and fewer individuals with humanist, intellectual, or political commitments entered the discipline. As early as thirty years ago the president of the American Psychoanalytic Association commented on the unmistakable conformism of the newer psychoanalytic candidates; he was, however, careful not to criticize this development; it was "interesting" and "significant," but nothing more. The candidates of the 1920s and 1930s, he noted, were a "different breed from the current crop." The former tended to be highly original and individualistic. In contrast, the newer candidates are "normal" and conventional.

They are not so introspective, are inclined to read only the literature that is assigned . . . and wish to get through with the training requirements as rapidly as possible. Their interests are primarily clinical rather than research and theoretical. . . . This "normalizing" of the composition of the membership is an interesting and perhaps significant phenomenon in the development of psychoanalysis in this country.[10]

Nor was this official alone in registering the change. The analyst Maxwell Gitelson bemoaned the Americanization. By the 1930s, he stated, "the era of literary and Bohemian adventurings in the unconscious was coming to an end." The influx of new students and the establishment of American institutes broke the identification of psychoanalysis with Europe. "In effect, all this represented a turning away from what was looked upon as the intellectualistic tendencies of European analysis and a turning toward the pragmatism of medicine with which analysis now declared itself affiliated."[11]

Gitelson later expanded on what he called the "identity crisis" of American psychoanalysis. Unlike in Europe, psychoanalysis in the United States required no "movement" to overcome obstacles; rather it suffered from the opposite blessing. Warmly welcomed by the mental health disciplines and psychiatry it was rapidly assimilated into the mainstream; the price, however, was high—a loss of the unique contribution of psychoanalysis.[12] A survey in 1950 already confirmed that psychoanalysis was "no longer an out-group discipline, but one which has been integrated extensively within the field of psychiatry."[13]

Absorbed by the medical profession, translated into a dry scientific idiom, practiced by conventional and pragmatic doctors, psychoanalysis developed very differently in Chicago and Topeka in the 1940s and 1950s from the way it had in Vienna and Berlin in the 1920s. "I had moved from the psychoanalytic coffeehouses of Europe," stated Martin Grotjahn, as he reflected on his trek from Berlin to Topeka, "to the big American institutes of psychoanalysis. . . . This difference caused fateful confusions."[14] Inside these institutes psychoanalysis fattened into a quiet trade; the intellectual fervor, reforming zeal, and theoretical boldness of classical psychoanalysis were history.

The forces that guided Americanization can be roughly identified: professionalization and medicalization; the insecurity of refugee analysts; the gap between American and European culture, and—as cause and effect—the emergence of the neo-Freudians.

Together these forces defined a phenomenon as critical to psychoanalysis as to any body of thought—its transmission across generations. A cultural tradition that earns or retains a public vitality requires more than cogent texts. A corpus can be preserved in libraries or private book collections; texts may come alive for single individuals. To cross the line from a scholarly or marginal discourse, however, to a public and cultural presence, teachers and students must breathe life into texts. The pivotal teaching situation extends further than formal courses, classes, and institutions; it relies on the ineffable human moments—the contact of the enthusiasms, desires, and fears of teachers with the emotions of students.

Since the transmission of culture is a fragile affair, a thousand realities can nurture or injure it. Basic scientific knowledge cannot be lost; and even if temporarily blocked, it can eventually be recovered from texts. Other elements of culture —art, philosophy, and so forth—depend more heavily on emotional coloring and human contact. If a certain urgency is not communicated by teachers or does not resonate in students, these cultural impulses dissipate. Although these impulses are captured in texts and paintings, they become documents of past eras if they are not replenished by new generations of followers.

Americanization reached into this delicate arena where psychoanalytic culture is passed from generation to generation; precisely because the zone of transmission is so delicate a few small changes can radically alter its shape. For instance, European intellectuals and American doctors might teach, as well as perceive, the identical texts of Freud in very different fashions. Within a single generation some features of psychoanalytic culture may slip away, while others receive endless attention. The vigor of psychoanalysis thus ultimately depends on how it is taught and understood.

The professionalization of psychoanalysis cannot be detached from the general professionalization over the last century of American life. In the 1870s and 1880s some two hundred professional associations—from the American Forestry Association to the American Mathematical Society—were founded. The formation of professional groups did not simply signify an increase in specialized knowledge requiring technical training, it also represented the controlling, segmenting, and monopolizing of skills. As Burton J. Bledstein states in his *Culture of Professionalism,*

By professionalizing a sphere of American life such as poverty, criminality or disease, Mid-Victorians planned both to isolate and control the phenomenon. . . . Every sphere of American life came within the power of the Mid-Victorian professional to set apart, regulate and contain.[15]

New professional groups regularly demanded the sole accrediting rights for their specialty; dental associations wanted exclusive rights to accredit dentists; lawyers wanted to accredit lawyers; and so on. They justified this demand by its public and private benefits: they aimed to protect the community from incompetent practitioners. They also wanted to secure and expand their trade by regulating the market. This entailed establishing rites and rituals to limit the flow into the profession as well as fend off internal threats. As these organizations prospered, they dampened and channeled internal dissent.

Especially in recent decades, the economic incentives for professionalization must be acknowledged. Independent specialists or intellectuals formally unify or affiliate with universities. This tendency reflects the "cartelization" of the economy. Very simply, the independent producer lacks the capital and resources to survive in a mass economy. For the same reason that "mom and pop" grocery or hardware stores succumb to national chains, independent intellectuals or specialists are rendered obsolete by major institutions; they either affiliate with universities or national organizations, or they find themselves out of business. Moreover, in an atomized society, institutional affiliation confers identity and legitimacy.

# The Americanization of Psychoanalysis

Psychoanalysis in America has generally conformed to the pattern of professionalization. A sudden increase in interest, students, and analysts in the 1930s and 1940s led to the founding of new institutes, a reorganization of the national association, and efforts to gain sole accrediting rights. As Fenichel himself noted, the conviviality of the early years and the direct emotional ties to Freud were foreign to new generations of New York or Chicago analysts.

A single form dominated the professionalization of psychoanalysis: medicalization or the exclusion of nonmedical (lay) analysts. Almost from its beginnings in the United States, the Americans sought to confine psychoanalysis to medical doctors. Few issues provoked Freud more passionately than lay analysis; he relentlessly defended it. His reasoning was simple and prescient; monopolization by medical doctors would degrade psychoanalysis into a specialty. Freud wanted psychoanalysis to contribute to general knowledge and culture; he objected to medical doctors restricting it to therapy.

For Freud, this was not a tangential concern; the future of psychoanalysis depended on blocking its monopolization by the medical doctors. Against the widespread sentiment of analysts, Freud insisted that its medical use was only a fraction of psychoanalysis.

The use of analysis for the treatment of neuroses is only one of its applications; the future will perhaps show that it is not the most important one. . . . It would be wrong to sacrifice all the other applications to this single one, just because it touches on the circle of medical interests.[16]

Freud never wavered or doubted the danger from the doctors. After a seven-year interval, almost his first words to the American analyst Clarence P. Oberndorf were, "And tell me, what do you really have against lay analysis?"[17]

The history of psychoanalysis is often interpreted as the history of subservience to Freud. Yet on the issue of lay analysis, especially in the United States, the medical doctors defeated Freud. Frequently, the more orthodox the analysts, the more they fought against Freud. Freud did not mince words; his defeat jeopardized psychoanalysis. He called the American resolutions against lay analysis "an attempt at repression."[18] The doctors of repression repressed their science.

Several motives induced American analysts to exclude nonmedical practitioners. They believed psychoanalysis required medical expertise in order to distinguish somatic and psychological disorders. The lack of prestige besetting psychoanalysis in its earlier years grieved them. By limiting analysis to medical doctors they ensured its respectability. Nor can the more cynical motives be discounted: eliminating the lay practitioners guaranteed them a larger and more lucrative trade. Walter C. Langer, himself a lay analyst trained in Vienna, reflected bitterly on the American hostility to lay analysts.

When I think of [lay] analysts like Anna Freud, Ernst Kris, Robert Waelder, Erik Erikson, to name only a few, I wonder what more they can expect. Confidentially, I sort of had the feeling that the early medical analysts who were instrumental in formulating the policies of our American institutes considered it a most effective way of closing the door to competition. . . . I cannot help but think back on the remark that the President of the New York Psychoanalytic Society made when I approached him for affidavits [for refugee analysts fleeing Vienna for the United States]: "What in the world would we do with all these additional analysts?"[19]

The exclusion of lay analysts not only confined analytic practice to medical doctors, it also delivered psychoanalysis to the medical establishment. Taught by doctors to interns, psychoanalysis became part of the medical curriculum. Moreover,

# The Americanization of Psychoanalysis

North American medical students, unlike their European counterparts, generally receive only a feeble humanist education; even before they are medical students, they often enroll in narrow premedical programs geared to winning a slot in medical schools. Medical education itself does not correct but intensifies this imbalance.[20] By the time doctors specialize in psychiatry, only the medical surface of psychoanalysis has any relevance or meaning to them.

More serious than the medical content of psychoanalytic education, medicalization acted as a human filter; it preselected the pool of potential psychoanalysts. Insofar as the competition to enter medical schools is keen, and the financial rewards often large, American medicine attracts the more conventional and conservative students. Few individuals with humanist or political designs enter the profession, and obviously few are available to enter psychoanalysis. When the first and second generation of Europeans studied psychoanalysis, they were not guaranteed a secure trade; rather they chose a risky new field, because of their devotion to its cultural, social, or personal implications. Many refugee analysts were embarrassed by the large fees they could, and were expected to, command in the United States.

This screening of psychoanalytic candidates may be the gravest consequence of medicalization, since the individuals who constitute a discipline predetermine its evolution. If these individuals are largely pragmatic and conservative doctors, they will impart these values to their profession, effectively insulating psychoanalysis from wider cultural currents. Moreover, the process tends to be self-perpetuating. Conventional doctors cast a science in their own image; this image becomes the reality which attracts new recruits who are in tune with a technical and prosperous trade.

Joel Kovel describes his analytic training recalling

the younger analysts fawning on the illuminati, those elder training analysts with seerlike access to privileged code words: "intrasystemic," "aggressivized energy," "deneutralization". . . . The main issues were complexity and a sterile field. Analysts should do nothing else but analysis, and analysis was nothing but a fantastically subtle and complex technical pursuit that related to nothing else in the world and was incomprehensible to the uninitiated, i.e., the whole population except for a thousand or so properly certified professionals. Thus was the outside kept out and the inside in.[21]

The medical filter not only sifted out mavericks, dissenters, intellectuals, humanists, and other "irregular" individuals, it also proved extremely effective in eliminating women. Historically medicine in the United States has been almost exclusively a male preserve. The proportion of female physicians (to male physicians) in the United States is one of the lowest in the world, around 7 percent in the 1960s. This figure is far below the average in Europe (except for Spain).[22] Moreover, American female physicians usually specialize in pediatrics. Obviously very few are even available to enter psychoanalytic training, resulting in a dearth of female analysts.

This contrasts dramatically with the situation of classical psychoanalysis; it is almost possible to speak of the "defeminization" of analysis. Not only were women a sizable presence in European analysis, from Lou Andreas-Salomé to Sabina Spielrein, Melanie Klein, Edith Jacobson, and Helene Deutsch, it also attracted exceptional women. As a new field dealing with sexuality, psychoanalysis drew women who were bucking the tide. It does not seem fortuitous that Fenichel's own circle of political analysts consisted—with a single exception—only of women. A more reliable index may be Fenichel's Children's Seminar, which was frequented by the more independent psychoanalytic candidates. According to Fenichel's roster of the forty-six analysts who participated, almost half were women.

In the United States, on the other hand, with few female

physicians, and lay analysis virtually prohibited, new women analysts are a rarity. Laura Fermi in her study of "intellectual" immigrants of the 1930s noted the sharp change. She compiled a list of almost two thousand intellectual immigrants, or refugees; her figures not only registered the preponderance of female analysts in Europe, but also their precipitous decline in number in America.

> A striking feature of the psychoanalytic wave [of immigrants] is the large number of women who formed a part of it: about 30 per cent of all analysts in my file are women. This is an extremely high proportion, not since maintained: in 1958 . . . women accounted for only 9 per cent of all students [in approved psychoanalytic institutes].[23]

Next to the quiet, if effective, process of medicalization, the impact of immigration was noisy and catastrophic. The analysts born around 1900 fled their homelands in the middle of their lives and careers. The power of psychoanalytic organizations to regulate dissent—or filter out dissenters—paled in comparison to the might of the state to expel or allow entry. Nor did doors swing open to central European, predominantly Jewish, exiles. Professing unpopular political opinions did not help matters. It was news to no one that the United States did not look kindly upon socialists and Marxists.

The refugees knew the risks. One relative of Fenichel's, arrested by the Gestapo, admitted to membership in the Communist party; Fenichel learned the lesson of valuing life over honesty. In one way or another, all the exiles came to this conclusion. As they filled out their applications for entry permits and visas, their politics evaporated; and what they left off the forms, they dumped in the Atlantic as they crossed it. When they arrived in the new world, their past belonged to the past.

The history of the psychoanalytic exiles is a short course on

American immigration. "The intellectual immigrants of the thirties . . . became Americanized at a much faster pace than any previous group of immigrants."[24] Highly educated, professional, and politically alert, they did not wish to threaten their precarious legal status by publicly, even privately, recalling their European political commitments. Within a very few years, often their children, students, friends, and new wives and husbands had only the vaguest inklings of their European years.

The fears of the immigrants were not ill-founded. Fenichel himself earned an FBI file. One good citizen reported to the FBI that "due to the fact that each and every German is now apparently under suspicion, I feel that I should give you the information . . . " He volunteered the damning information that Fenichel seemed very anxious about receiving his mail; even worse the mail was in German. A more professional account was submitted by an FBI "special agent" in Los Angeles under the heading "Espionage." "In May 1938, one *Otto Fenichel* moved into the premises at. . . . This man gave out that he was a psychoanalyst." The agent attached a description which completed the portrait of Fenichel as a spy: "*Hair:* dark, bushy; *Eyes:* dark—wears glasses; *Complexion:* dark and swarthy; *Nose:* prominent; *Nationality:* possibly of German extraction."[25] Fenichel believed that his naturalization was delayed because of his political past.

Only the foolhardy would parade their political loyalties in this situation. The cold war and McCarthyism intimidated any who hoped that a postwar America might liberalize the political atmosphere. For a generation that had its family, friends, and patients arrested, and often killed, this was sufficient intimidation. To this day many refugees remain politically circumspect.

The consequences of these fears are incalculable: they affected the projects, the vocabulary, and the thoughts of the refugees. In reducing—usually eliminating—their public profiles, the political Freudians jeopardized the transmission of their knowledge, ideas, and commitments. Insofar as they did not present themselves as political or oppositional thinkers, they could not attract kindred souls or students. Their secrecy and caution ensured their personal survival, even success, but ultimately ensured their cultural demise; they were unable to pass along their ideas to a new generation.

A comparison with the Frankfurt School may be instructive here. The Frankfurt School also advanced political and nonconformist perspectives in their "critical theory." They enjoyed however a very different fate: from Walter Benjamin to T. W. Adorno, they became essential reference points of contemporary culture. Although they proceeded cautiously, as did the political Freudians, they also preserved a public identity, partly by toning down their radicalism. As Henry Pachter caustically observed: "They said alienation when they meant capitalism, reason when they meant revolution, and Eros when they meant proletariat. In this way they hoped to assure Marxist philosophy an underground survival during the McCarthy episode."[26]

Within these cautious limits, members of the Frankfurt School ran their own institute, and, until 1941, they edited their own journal which—to be sure—was hardly known in the United States. They also published works that expressed their commitments, often in Aesopian language. A minor clash with Simmel illustrated their sensitivity to losing their identity. Adorno protested when he discovered that the volume that Simmel was editing, *Anti-Semitism*, to which they all had contributed (Adorno, Horkheimer, Fenichel, Simmel, and others) was to be dedicated to President Roosevelt. Adorno felt that this was an obvious ploy, playing up an Americanism that they did not possess.[27]

By refusing to completely submerge their identity as "critical" thinkers, the Frankfurt School theorists were able to teach a new generation of students who by the 1960s infused life into their works. By contrast, Fenichel and the political Freudians preserved a secrecy that took its revenge: the transmission— the very survival—of their knowledge across the generations was disrupted.

The limits, perhaps the invalidity, of this comparison illuminates the obstacles that faced the political Freudians: it is unfair to compare an institute and an informal collection of individuals. The Frankfurt School was funded, edited its own journal, and sponsored a series of publications. Moreover, by virtue of its resources, it could maintain a geographical center —Frankfurt, New York, Los Angeles. This enabled key individuals to remain together to collaborate. Geographic proximity may be a minimal condition for creating a body of literature with a distinct identity. There is simply no substitute for frequent meetings of individuals with similar ideas. In contrast, exile scattered the political Freudians across the globe. With the loss of a geographic hub they may have lost the possibility of an identity. Of course this was the *raison d'être* of the *Rundbriefe,* but it was a poor replacement, as Fenichel complained, for actual discussions.

In addition, the brevity of Fenichel's life may also invalidate any comparison. Fenichel was the animating force of the political Freudians. If he had lived longer he might have galvanized the oppositional analysts. During the war, indeed through the mid-1950s, the Frankfurt School maintained its lowest profile; for instance, during this period, Herbert Marcuse and Franz Neumann worked for the United States government. To put it another way, if the Frankfurt School theorists—like the political Freudians all born around 1900—had neither published nor taught after 1946, the year of Fenichel's death, it is certain their contributions would today be little known.

Inasmuch as the political Freudians did not intrude on the

public consciousness, they left a vacancy that the neo-Freudians successfully occupied. The neo-Freudian revisionists garnered an audience a more public political Freudianism might have tapped. In accessible prose, Fromm, Horney, and others mounted a cultural and social critique which became almost conventional wisdom. Adopted by many social scientists and repeated in scores of college courses, it maintains that psychoanalysis was a creaking nineteenth-century dogma suffering from pansexualism, panbiologism, and panhistoricism.

Against this flood the political Freudians did not establish an independent public position. Fenichel developed a stringent theoretical critique of the neo-Freudians; however, it never gained much currency—or did so only when elaborated in Frankfurt School texts such as Marcuse's *Eros and Civilization*. The secrecy of the political Freudians again rendered any published critique an isolated sally with no literature to support it.

Moreover the political Freudians assumed an alliance with the conservative Freudians that swallowed up any remaining public visibility. The relationship among the conservative, political, and neo-Freudians is a case study of the complexity of translating theoretical disputes into practical agreements. The organizational coalitions drowned the theoretical issues that prompted the coalition.

To the casual traveler in the 1940s and 1950s, the psychoanalytic landscape appeared to break down into two different terrains: a complacent and technical orthodoxy restricted to doctors; and looser revisionism that encouraged cultural and moral theorizing. That the landscape harbored some unmarked caves did not matter; they did not suffice to attract intellectual spelunkers. Without markers or teachers, the political Freudians languished in the shadows of the conservatives.

However flawed their oeuvre, the neo-Freudians successfully and publicly staked out a social and cultural turf. With some notable exceptions, such as the rank reductionism and anticommunism of W. R. D. Fairbairn,[28] they offered a broad social theorizing. At every point in his career Fromm entertained humanist, political, and religious issues; and even Horney appealed to the tradition of Wilhelm Reich and referred to Max Horkheimer.[29] By parading their cultural commitments, the neo-Freudians captured an audience repelled by the conservatism and reductionism of a medical orthodoxy.

Their unhappy alliance with conservative psychoanalysis rendered the political Freudians invisible. Fenichel regretted this tactical constellation, but he was impaled by the logic of revisionism and orthodoxy. Social blindness and reductionism afflicted psychoanalytic orthodoxy; nevertheless the neo-Freudians adulterated psychoanalysis into a vague idealism and flat sociology. Fenichel appreciated their cultural and social impulses, but he could not accept the revisions that excised the heart from psychoanalysis. The position was theoretically cogent and organizationally invisible. Fenichel looked for allies from Hans Sachs to Paul Goodman,[30] but a public opposition did not survive.

"These have been the years of conformity and depression. A stench of fear has come out of every pore of American life," wrote Norman Mailer in 1957, "and we suffer from a collective failure of nerve. The only courage, with rare exceptions, that we have been witness to, has been the isolated courage of isolated people."[31] By the 1950s a cold-war consensus, propped up by prosperity and enforced by McCarthyism, discouraged intellectual dissent. It was a period to celebrate American genius, pluralism, and democracy. Challenges to the culture belonged to the past, the 1930s, or to the future, the 1960s.

The conformism of the wider society weighed heavily on professionals whose jobs and advancement depended on the approval of colleagues and superiors. C. Wright Mills, like

Mailer a maverick, decried "the political failure of intellectual nerve" that afflicted the culture. His *White Collar* (1951) blamed a bureaucratization for transforming intellectuals into technocrats and entrepreneurs. The professional—and professor—lost the motive and ability to resist the conventions; they became subdued intellectual pieceworkers.[32]

The 1950s exacted a toll on intellectual life. This observation, however, risks degenerating into self-congratulations, as if today we are bold and nonconformist. Nevertheless the 1950s did not nurture dissent. After the great Depression and war, prosperity allowed the pursuit or resumption of normal family life and careers. Along with other professionals, psychoanalysts joined in; and the discipline as a whole gained students, recognition, and medical respectability.

It also suffered a dulling of vision and vitality. The words of Clarence P. Oberndorf, one of the earliest American analysts, register the advances, but they also serve as an indictment. "Psychoanalysis had finally become legitimate and respectable," he wrote in 1953, "perhaps paying the price in becoming sluggish and smug, hence attractive to an increasing number of minds which find security in conformity and propriety."[33] By one of the pioneers of American psychoanalysis these words are damning. Yet the price may have been higher than anyone suspected; in the 1950s the last links to a classical psychoanalysis snapped.

Almost every discipline at any particular time harbors independent people. It is a mistake to paint the 1950s in excessively gray tones as if no one bucked the decade. Not only the "beats" and literary figures such as Norman Mailer but isolated rebels survived in all the professions, including psychoanalysis. Yet psychoanalysis proceeded further on the path of repression, so neutralizing its own rebels that it irreparably damaged its intellectual vitality. To examine briefly the fate of several of these rebels of the 1950s sharpens the portrait of psychoanalysis. The work of Paul Baran, C. Wright Mills, and Robert Lindner drew on different traditions and addressed dissimilar audiences. Nevertheless, their impact on their respective disciplines illuminates the peculiar situation of psychoanalysis.

In the late 1940s and early 1950s, Paul Baran in economics, C. Wright Mills in sociology, and Robert Lindner in psychoanalysis mined as well as reinvented a dissenting literature. Each suffered from an almost visceral isolation. Allies were few and far between, and their professions and institutions proved inhospitable. Baran frequently complained with bitterness of his treatment by Stanford University; much of his life Mills railed against universities and the sociology profession; and Lindner, a lay analyst, overcame the resistance of his local psychoanalytic society (Washington-Baltimore) to practice psychoanalysis. It is perhaps not accidental that none of them lived a full life, each dying of heart disease. Baran died at the age of fifty-four in 1964; Mills died at forty-six in 1962; and Lindner died at forty-one in 1956.

The writings of Baran and Mills have become fundamental texts and references in economics and sociology.[34] Today their books, Baran's *Political Economy of Growth* and *Monopoly Capital* (written with Paul Sweezy) and Mills's *White Collar, The Power Elite,* and other works, are almost required reading in their fields; they spark instant recognition by economists and sociologists. A sizable literature examines their contributions, and currently, their students and disciples are active and influential. Many internal critiques of economics and sociology are founded on the oeuvre of Baran and Mills.

To turn to Lindner is a different story. Some may recognize his name but know little more about him, although several of his books, in particular *The Fifty-Minute Hour*, currently in its thirty-third printing, remain very successful.[35] This is his most "neutral" work, a presentation of five case studies with minimal theorizing. That Lindner was a rebel, a dissenting analyst, and often a trenchant social critic has passed out of the collective —and psychoanalytic—consciousness.

Lindner may be most famous for his first book, *Rebel without a Cause* (1944), since its title (and little else) was used in the movie of the same name; he also shared the fate of early death that struck all the principals of the film (James Dean, Sal Mineo, and Natalie Wood). His first writings drew on his profession of prison psychologist at a federal penitentiary. *Rebel without a Cause* is a long case study of a single prisoner. In his introduction, Lindner states that the criminal "psychopath" is a "rebel without a cause, an agitator without a slogan, a revolutionary without a program."[36] His next book, *Stone Walls and Men* (1946), argues for prison reform.[37]

An able writer, Lindner's success owed to his skill at presenting case material, both in *Rebel without a Cause* and *The Fifty-Minute Hour*. In his less popular books, *Prescription for Rebellion* (1952) and *Must You Conform?* (1956), Lindner assumes the stance of a psychoanalytic critic of society. The idiom and references diverge from those of the political Freudians, but he shares with them a spirit and orientation. Lindner transformed his study of rebels "without a cause" into an advocacy of rebellion with a cause. For Lindner, all psychology, and indeed all society, conspire in promoting adjustment. Years before it became a popular cause, Lindner relentlessly attacked shock treatment and brain surgery as scandalous methods of pacifying recalcitrant patients.

Lindner came closest to Fenichel in his critique of the neo-Freudians: he decried the hymn to adjustment that pervaded their work; and, like Fenichel, he charged that the neo-Freudians diluted psychoanalysis into a weak sociology by surrendering its instinctual base. In casting off the animal, carnal, and erotic dimensions of life, they depleted the sources of rebellion; they lacked a psychic and theoretical external point from which to mount a critique of society. To be sure, Lindner did not believe that the instincts were strictly biological; they were both biological and psychological. The "pervasive fear and distrust" of instincts, however, were part and parcel of the cult of passivity and adjustment. To affirm instinct is to "range oneself squarely against domestication."[38]

Lindner sharply attacks as proponents of a conformist psychology Fromm, Horney, Adler and Sullivan. Horney, he believes, is "the most obvious of the supporters of adjustment and domestication, and her views provide a defense against the often disturbing, discomforting Freudian theses." With its "ring of modernity," her work has won its way into "the hearts of sociologists and anthropologists." For them she has renounced the "preoccupation with sex." She speaks in

terms a red-blooded, clean-minded, go-getting American can understand. We have always thought that anyone who is different from us is queer, and Horney by her "scientific" exposition of neuroses as marked essentially by deviation from the regnant cultural pattern, now supports this which we have always known.[39]

It does not seem accidental that Lindner was a lay analyst and a fierce critic of medicalization. He believed that the "relative stagnation" of psychoanalysis and psychotherapy of "this generation of practitioners as compared with the abundantly productive last generation" was due "almost exclusively to the insistence upon the prerequisite of a medical education for a license to practice." Pragmatic and technical medical schools only half educate doctors. "In the place of broad systemized knowledge of man, his culture and his works, this majority [of medical practitioners] possesses a handful of clinical facts wrapped about with terminological vagaries." Lindner warned that if the situation were not reversed the "medically pure practitioners will suffer from the sterility and debility which is the price of isolation."[40]

# The Americanization of Psychoanalysis

Lindner broadened his critique of American psychoanalysis into a barrage against American society. Every sector and every discipline—education, counseling, welfare, psychology—fostered adjustment and passivity. He was neither sanguine nor stoical; he viewed the individual as completely outgunned and outmaneuvered. "Today in the struggle between man and Society over the issue of conformity, Society is winning."

In many ways Lindner's work was flawed. A shrill, sometimes apocalyptic tone marred his best efforts; he seemed convinced that only a few moments remained before conformity would snuff out the last remnants of humanity. Rallying to Ortega y Gasset's *Revolt of the Masses* (1930), he almost embraced an elitist cultural philosophy, lamenting the rise of the "mass man." Moreover, a very conventional anticommunism weakened his critique of society. The critic of conformist psychology was convinced that "the mystery of communism's appeal can be solved only by psychology."[41]

The cause of Lindner's very limited, perhaps nonexistent, impact on psychoanalysis may derive from the deficiencies of his work, its inadequate breadth and depth. Pieced together out of too many disparate parts, it failed to cohere. In addition, its shrillness and overdramatization set it outside normal scholarly discourse. If Lindner was frequently on target, his mode and style rendered him unpalatable to his psychoanalytic colleagues.

This may be true, but superficial. For the deficiencies of Lindner's work may not be solely personal; they bear witness to an American psychoanalysis that had already repressed its past. To put it sharply, by the 1950s American psychoanalysis could only engender a flawed protest against itself. Classical psychoanalysis and even the political Freudians were beyond recall. For an American analyst educated in this period, the psychoanalytic resources for social theorizing were no longer available. Lindner was a psychoanalytic loner because the community of classic psychoanalytic theorists had dissipated, and, like any loner, in striking out by himself, he risked getting lost.

In contrast to Lindner, Baran and Mills found their way to the dense theoretical pasts of their disciplines. Baran, of course, was European born and educated, and he effortlessly employed classic European texts. Partly through the influence of émigré scholars such as Hans Gerth, Mills, a Texan, imbibed Marx, Weber and the Frankfurt School writings. Lindner was less fortunate. He did not find his way because there was no way; the path had slipped out of sight and mind.

Lindner signified a final and eloquent protest against the impoverishment of American psychoanalysis. He was also its victim insofar as he lacked access to its classical and political traditions; consequently his protest was shot through by its object, domesticated psychoanalysis. At the time of his death, psychoanalysis flourished, but it flourished as a decultured trade. When Fenichel fled Europe he pledged to himself not to surrender the heart and soul of classical analysis; indeed this was the program of the political Freudians—to hold fast to the raw power of psychoanalysis. This program, these hopes, did not survive Americanization; they sank into the unconscious of the profession.

# APPENDIX

# Four *Rundbriefe*

AS a sample of the style and contents of the *Rundbriefe,* I outline four letters, selected almost at random, with two from the early period and two from the late period.

1) Letter XIII (4 April 1935) runs thirteen pages. Its first three items deal with the group's publications. In item 1 Fenichel states that he has just sent out several of his manuscripts to members of the circle who have not yet seen them, and that he is preparing a critique of Laswell's *Psychopathology and Politics.* Item 2 announces Fenichel's decision to submit for publication his recent lecture on pedagogy, "The Means of Education." Item 3 states that he has completed a reply to a recent attack against Wilhelm Reich. These first three items consume less than a page. Items 4, 5, and 6 form the bulk of the letter, almost ten pages, and consist of a lengthy account of a visit with Reich, a letter from that visitor, and an extract from a pronouncement against Reich. The last items are again brief. Item 7 notes an incisive attack on Jung, and inquires whether anyone knows its author, Walter Hartmann. In item 8, referring to some recent publications, Fenichel comments that Anna Freud has begun in a "salutary way the struggle against Melanie Klein in English." Edith Jacobson provides the latest news in item 9 about the neo-Nazi line introduced into the Berlin Institute, and item 10 notes that a lecture on

Hitler, which Fenichel is trying to obtain, has been delivered to the London Psychoanalytic Society.

2) Three weeks later Fenichel mailed out letter XIV (26 April 1935), consisting of nine pages. Item 1 announces that Fenichel has sent out his Laswell critique and hopes everyone circulates it. Item 2 notes the appearance of the latest official psychoanalytic journal with the report of the Lucerne Congress from which Reich was excluded. The full account of the debate and exclusion, which had been promised Reich and Fenichel, has been completely suppressed; and in the official account of the congress, Fenichel comments with some disbelief, the major debate is not mentioned. In item 3 Fenichel states that he has not yet heard from Waelder (concerning his response to Waelder), but Waelder's own "anti-Marxist bourgeois sociology" continues to be well represented in *Imago*. Item 4 is devoted to exchanges with Edward Glover, provoked by Fenichel's critical review of Glover's *War, Sadism, and Pacifism*. Glover replied to the published review and sent the reply ("Fenichel's main criticisms . . . represent the conventional reply of the socialist or communist to any psychological approach which appears to threaten his pet economic and sociological theories") with a cover note to Fenichel, who counterreplied. Brief critical surveys of recent psychoanalytic literature constitute items 5 and 6, while item 7 provides a two-page summary of the lecture on Hitler Fenichel mentioned in his earlier letter with a copy of his letter to its author. Item 8 gives a short account of a German conference on psychotherapy (Jung's star seems to be "sinking"). Items 9 and 10 are devoted to some questions and answers, for example, does anyone know something about Harry S. Sullivan? and Hartmann, referred to in letter XIII, is a pseudonym for a Paris-based author. Excerpts of reviews from a psychoanalytic journal appear in item 11, and item 12 encourages everyone to reply to past *Rundbriefe* and to circulate manuscripts.

## Appendix: Four *Rundbriefe*

3) Six and half years later Fenichel sent out Letter 80 (3 September 1941), twenty-five pages long. Item 1 discusses for five pages the "paradox" of the Karen Horney opposition to the establishment. Like their circle her group also objects to the neglect of social factors by orthodox psychoanalysis and institutes; but since she is renouncing Freud, Fenichel believes his group must side with the official organization. Item 2 notes that Theodor Reik has founded his own organization. Items 3 and 4 are short reports on activities in Los Angeles and San Francisco, and item 5 quotes from a letter to an unnamed recipient that calls Fenichel's attitude on psychoanalytic matters "quite conservative. . . . We ought to have somebody defend the more radical points of view." Item 6 announces a new publication by Kate Friedländer and item 7 consists of a lengthy review by J. C. Flugel of several books, including Mannheim's *Man and Society in an Age of Reconstruction.* In items 8 and 9 Fenichel presents a review he wrote on a booklet on psychological warfare and an academic essay on social psychology.

4) Three weeks later (27 September 1941) Fenichel sent out Letter 81, ten pages long. The first four items provide news of Anna Freud's activities in London; Edith Jacobson and Annie Reich's lectures in New York; the absence of "opposition" to Alexander in Chicago; and conflicts in California over the proposed constitution for the new psychoanalytic society. Item 5 excerpts a letter reporting the psychoanalytic situation in Argentina; item 6 abstracts a recent Fenichel lecture; and item 7 reports that the U.S. Department of Coordination of Information seeks to enlist psychoanalysis in the war effort. Fenichel comments that it is "sad" how little it can offer. In item 8, Martin Grotjahn responds to a review by Fenichel critical of Glover. Finally, items 9 and 10 concern publications by Franz Alexander and Sandor Rado.

# NOTES

THE PAPERS and *Rundbriefe* of Otto Fenichel's to which I had access are largely in private hands; the bulk are in the possession of Randi Markowitz; others were made available to me by Dr. Emanuel Windholz and Prof. Hanna Fenichel Pitkin. Some of Fenichel's papers are included with Siegfried Bernfeld's at the YIVO Institute for Jewish Research in New York. Ernst Simmel's papers are located in the Library of the Los Angeles Psychoanalytic Society and Institute and in special collections of the University of California, Los Angeles, library. I consulted transcribed oral histories at the Abraham A. Brill Library of the New York Psychoanalytic Institute, the Oral Research Office of Columbia University, and the library of the Los Angeles Psychoanalytic Society and Institute. I conducted personal interviews with Rudolf Ekstein, Lawrence J. Friedman, Henry and Yela Lowenfeld, George Gero, Miriam Williams, Martin Grotjahn, Clare Fenichel, and Norman Reider. I exchanged letters with numerous other analysts or their families. In general I have cited these sources—interviews and letters—sparingly in the notes.

CHAPTER ONE / The Repression of Psychoanalysis

1. Martin Freud, *Sigmund Freud: Man and Father* (New York: Vanguard, 1958), p. 205.

2. Ernest Jones, *The Life and Work of Sigmund Freud*, 3 vols. (New York: Basic Books, 1953–57), 3: 218 (hereafter cited as Jones, *Freud*, 1, 2, or 3).

3. See Dieter Wagner and Gerhard Tomkowitz, *Anschluss: The Week Hitler Seized Vienna* (New York: St. Martin's, 1971).

4. Jones, *Freud*, 3: 226.

# Notes

5. Reuben Fine, *A History of Psychoanalysis* (New York: Columbia University Press, 1979), pp. 111–12.

6. Sigmund Freud, "The Uncanny," *Collected Papers*, 5 vols. (London: Hogarth Press, 1957), 4:394.

7. Freud, "On the History of the Psychoanalytic Movement," *Collected Papers* (London, 1957), 1:297.

8. Helene Deutsch, *Confrontations with Myself* (New York: Norton, 1973), p. 131.

9. Fine, *History of Psychoanalysis*, p. 108.

10. Edward Kronold, "Edith Jacobson 1897–1978," *Psychoanalytic Quarterly* 49 (1980): 505–7.

11. Peter Blos, "Berta Bornstein 1899–1971," in *The Psychoanalytic Study of the Child*, ed. R. Eissler et al. (New Haven: Yale University Press, 1974), 29:36.

12. Edith Jacobson, "Annie Reich (1902–1971)," *International Journal of Psychoanalysis* 52 (1971): 334.

13. Sigmund Freud, "The Goethe Prize," in *Standard Edition of the Complete Works of Sigmund Freud* (London: Hogarth Press, 1961), 21: 205–12. See also Alfons Paquet, "Zum Goethe-Preis 1930," *Die Psychoanalytische Bewegung* 2 (1930): 426–30. This same volume of the *Die Psychoanalytische Bewegung* contains several articles discussing Freud as a prose stylist: Walter Musch, "Freud als Schriftsteller," pp. 467–509 and Hermann Hesse et al., "Freuds Sprache," pp. 510–11.

14. Thomas Mann, "Freud and the Future" (1936), in *Essays of Three Decades*, trans. H. T. Lowe-Porter (New York: Knopf, 1948), pp. 411–28.

15. Nathan G. Hale, Jr., *Freud and the Americans* (New York: Oxford University Press, 1971). See also John Burnham, *Psychoanalysis and American Medicine 1894–1918*, Psychological Issues Monograph Series, no. 20. (New York: International Universities Press, 1967).

16. Nathan G. Hale, Jr., "From Berggasse XIX to Central Park West: The Americanization of Psychoanalysis, 1919–1940," *Journal of the History of the Behavioral Sciences* 14 (1978): 306.

17. Robert Michels, *Political Parties* (1911; reprint New York: Dover, 1959).

18. For a survey of the personal relations between Freud and various Social Democrats, as well as an encyclopedic overview of Austro-Marxism, see Ernst Glaser, *Im Umfeld des Austromarxismus* (Vienna: Europaverlag, 1981), esp. pp. 259–72.

19. Freud to Julie-Braun Vogelstein (30 October 1927), in Martin Grotjahn, "A Letter by Sigmund Freud with Recollections of his Adolescence," *Journal of the American Psychoanalytic Association* 4 (1956):648.

20. Grotjahn, "A Letter by Sigmund Freud," p. 644.

21. Ronald Florence, *Fritz: The Story of a Political Assassin* (New York:

# Notes

Dial Press, 1971), p. 3. For additional information on Freud and Braun see Hugo Knoepfmacher, "Sigmund Freud in High School," *American Imago* 36 (1979): 294–96.

22. See William J. McGrath, "Freud as Hannibal: The Politics of the Brother Band," *Central European History* 7 (1974):39–40. The links between the Social Democratic Adlers and Freud seem endless. Richard F. Sterba recounts in his recent memoirs that a discussion with one of Victor Adler's sons—apparently Karl Adler, Friedrich's brother—first stimulated his interest in Freud (*Reminiscences of a Viennese Psychoanalyst* [Detroit: Wayne State University Press, 1982], p. 19).

23. Fredric Wertham, review of *The Psychoanalytic Theory of Neurosis* by Otto Fenichel, *The New Republic* (27 May 1946):780.

24. Bruno Bettelheim, "Freud and the Soul," *New Yorker*, 1 March 1982, p. 52.

25. H. Nunberg and E. Federn, eds., *Minutes of the Vienna Psychoanalytic Society*, vol. 4:*1912–1918* (New York: International Universities Press, 1975), pp. 296–99.

26. Out of a massive literature on Lukács, see Andrew Arato and Paul Breines, *The Young Lukács and the Origin of Western Marxism* (New York: Seabury, 1979). See also David Kettler, "Culture and Revolution: Lukács in the Hungarian Revolution of 1918," *Telos* 10 (Winter 1971):35–92, which depicts the atmosphere of Budapest out of which both Lukács and Mannheim emerged. See my *Dialectic of Defeat: Contours of Western Marxism* (New York: Cambridge University Press, 1981).

27. Barbara Lantos, "Julia Mannheim 1895–1955," *International Journal of Psychoanalysis* 37 (1956):197–98.

28. Otto Friedrich, *Before the Deluge: A Portrait of Berlin in the 1920's* (New York: Avon Books, 1973), p. 24.

29. Barbara Lantos lived half of her time in Leipzig.

30. Interview with Martin Grotjahn, Los Angeles, 25 October 1980.

31. Jones, *Freud*, 2:152–53.

32. Martin Grotjahn has written a commentary on the "Rundbriefe" of the Committee: "Notes on Reading the 'Rundbriefe,' " *Journal of the Otto Rank Association* 8 (1973–74): 35–88. According to Dr. Grotjahn, whose source was Franz Alexander, the existence of these letters was a "well-kept secret" until the Jones biography (Grotjahn to Jacoby, 27 July 1981).

33. I refer to the *Rundbriefe* using Fenichel's own system, citing in parentheses letter number/date/section number. The first seventy-three letters were assigned roman numerals; and the remainder were in Arabic. Each letter was dated and subdivided into numbered sections. Under the best of conditions, a fourth or fifth carbon copy on tissue paper is difficult

# Notes

to read; after a half century legibility sharply declines. Moreover the copies to which I had access were rarely afforded the best of treatment, having been packed, repacked, and ignored during the wanderings of the recipients. Many are missing and many are decayed and unreadable. Where, as was often the case, the top sheet of a letter was missing, I have guessed at its date and indicate this in the citation by a question mark next to the letter number, date, or section number to signal my uncertainty. Unfortunately, I have had to guess at other matters as well: sometimes the texts themselves were difficult to decipher. The absence of sheets or letters may also have affected my overall interpretation. When or if other letters or pages show up reinterpretation might be possible or necessary. Finally, the first seventy letters are mainly in German with the remainder mainly in English. Unless otherwise indicated, the translations are my own. Fenichel's own English was imperfect, and his English publications were closely edited by friends; for this reason I have occasionally made minor changes in the English of his unpublished writings.

34. For some recent reflections see Peter Gay, "Encounter with Modernism: German Jews in Wilhelminian Culture," *Freud, Jews and Other Germans* (New York: Oxford University Press, 1979), pp. 93–168.

35. Ralph R. Greenson, "Otto Fenichel 1898–1946: The Encylopedia of Psychoanalysis," in *Psychoanalytic Pioneers*, ed. F. Alexander, S. Eisenstein, and M. Grotjahn (New York: Basic Books, 1966), p. 442. The birthdate given here, 1898, is incorrect.

36. Rudolph M. Loewenstein, "In Memorium: Otto Fenichel," *Psychoanalytic Quarterly* 15 (1946):140.

37. Bertram D. Lewin, "Introduction," in Otto Fenichel, *Collected Papers: First Series*, ed. H. Fenichel and D. Rapaport (New York: Norton, 1953), p. vii.

38. Alexander Grinstein, ed., *The Index of Psychoanalytic Writings* (New York: International Universities Press, 1956), 1:481–500.

39. "First Interview with Dr. Hanna Fenichel" by Dr. W. Horowitz (16 February 1963), Oral History, Los Angeles Psychoanalytic Society.

40. Apart from Greenson, Lewin, and Loewenstein, personal and published accounts include those of Norman Reider, "Otto Fenichel," *Dictionary of American Biography*, suppl. 4 (1946–1950) (New York: Scribner's, 1974), p. 264; Ernst Simmel, "Otto Fenichel," *International Journal of Psychoanalysis* 27 (1946):67–71; and Adelheid Koch, "Otto Fenichel," *Revista de Psicoanálisis* (Buenos Aires), (1946) 4:157–58.

41. Interview with Martin Grotjahn, Los Angeles, 19 October 1982; Greenson, "Otto Fenichel," p. 441.

# Notes

## Chapter Two / Spring's Awakening: Analysts as Rebels

1. T. W. Adorno, "Jene zwangziger Jahre," *Eingriffe* (Frankfurt: Suhrkamp, 1963), p. 59.

2. Sigmund Freud, "The Psychoanalytic Movement," *Collected Papers* (London: Hogarth Press, 1957), 1:350.

3. S. Freud, " 'Civilized' Sexual Morality and Modern Nervousness," *Collected Papers* (London: Hogarth Press, 1957), 2:99, 92–93.

4. S. Freud, *Five Lectures on Psychoanalysis*, trans. James Strachey (New York: Norton, 1977), pp. 54–55.

5. Gross cited Freud's remarks to him in "Ludwig Rubiners 'Psychoanalyse,' " *Die Aktion* 3 (14 May 1913): 507.

6. *Neue Wiener Journal*, 10 January 1914 as cited in Emanuel Hurwitz, *Otto Gross. 'Paradies'—Sucher zwischen Freud und Jung* (Zurich and Frankfurt: Suhrkamp 1979), pp. 14–15.

7. Franz Jung, "Der bekannte Kriminalprofessor Hans Gross in Graz," *Revolution* (1913). Reprinted in Jung's *Feinde Ringsum. Prosa und Aufsätze 1912 bis 1963*, ed. L. Schulenburg (Hamburg: Edition Nautilus, 1981), pp. 82–83.

8. Hans Gross, *Criminal Investigation*, 5th ed., ed. Richard L. Jackson (London: Sweet and Maxwell, 1962), p. x.

9. See generally Martin Green, *The Von Richthofen Sisters* (New York: Basic Books, 1974); compare Arthur Mitzman, "Anarchism, Expressionism and Psychoanalysis," *New German Critique* 10 (Winter, 1977): pp. 77–104.

10. Freud to Jung (19 April 1908) in *The Freud/Jung Letters*, ed. W. McGuire (Princeton: Princeton University Press, 1974), p. 141.

11. Ibid. (29 May 1908), p. 154.

12. Ernest Jones, *Free Associations* (London: Hogarth Press, 1959), pp. 173–74.

13. Franz Werfel, *The Pure in Heart*, trans. Geoffrey Dunlop (New York: Book League, 1931), pp. 347, 425, 561.

14. Jung to Freud (25 September 1907), *Freud/Jung Letters*, p. 90.

15. O. Gross, "Anmerkungen zu einer neuen Ethik," *Die Aktion* 3 (6 December 1913): 1141–42.

16. O. Gross, "Zur Überwindung der kulturellen Krise," *Die Aktion* 3 (2 April 1913): 385. See also Gross, "Protest und Moral im Unbewussten," *Die Erde*, vol. 1, no. 24 (15 December 1919), pp. 681–85.

17. O. Gross, "Zur Überwindung," p. 387.

18. Freud to Jung (25 February 1908), *Freud/Jung Letters*, p. 126.

19. Ibid. (19 May 1908), p. 152.

20. Jung to Freud (19 June 1908), *Freud/Jung Letters*, pp. 155–56.

21. Aldo Carotenuto, *A Secret Symmetry: Sabina Spielrein between Jung and Freud* (New York: Pantheon, 1982).

22. Spielrein to Freud (11 June 1909) in *Secret Symmetry*, p. 93.

23. Ibid. (? 1909), p. 107.

24. Jung to Freud (4 June 1909), *Freud/Jung Letters*, p. 229.

25. Franz Jung to Cläre Jung (15 April 1955) in Franz Jung, *Der Tolle Nikolaus. Prose, Briefe*, ed. Cläre Jung and F. Mierau (Frankfurt: Röderberg Verlag, 1981), pp. 369–70.

26. Frieda Lawrence to Harry T. Moore (14 January 1955) in F. Lawrence, *The Memoirs and Correspondence*, ed. E. W. Tedlock, Jr. (New York: Knopf, 1964), p. 388.

27. See generally my *Social Amnesia: A Critique of Conformist Psychology from Adler to Laing* (Boston: Beacon Press, 1975). Although Freud rightly denounced Adlerian psychology as "reactionary and retrogressive," its social accents did attract educational reformers and socialists. See Manès Sperber, *Masks of Loneliness: Alfred Adler in Perspective* (New York: Macmillan, 1974) for the memoirs of one left-wing Adlerian; also see Gottfried Mergner, *Arbeiterbewegung und Intelligenz* (Starnberg: Werner Raith, 1973) for an account of Otto Ruhle, the most interesting of the left-wing Adlerians. For Federn, see my *Social Amnesia* and Rudolf Ekstein, "Reflections on and Translation of Paul Federn's 'The Fatherless Society,'" *Reiss-Davis Clinic Bulletin* 8 (Spring 1971): 2–33.

28. Richard L. Rubenstein, *The Cunning of History* (New York: Harper & Row, 1978), p. 7.

29. Stefan Zweig, *The World of Yesterday*, introduction by Harry Zohn (Lincoln, Nebraska: University of Nebraska Press, 1964), p. 226.

30. Ibid., pp. 1–2.

31. The basic work remains Walter Z. Laqueur, *Young Germany: A History of the German Youth Movement* (London: Routledge and Kegan Paul, 1962). See also Harry Pross, *Jugend. Eros. Politik. Die Geschichte der deutschen Jugendverbände* (Bern: Schwerz Verlag, 1964); Robert Wohl, *The Generation of 1914* (Cambridge, Mass.: Harvard University Press, 1979), pp. 42 [ff.]. A basic anthology is Werner Kindt, ed., *Grundschriften der deutschen Jugendbewegung* (Düsseldorf: Eugen Diederichs Verlag, 1963). Bernhard Schneider, *Daten zur Geschichte der Jugendbewegung* (Bad Godesberg: Voggenreiter Verlag, 1965).

32. On scouting, see John Springhall, *Youth, Empire and Society: British Youth Movements, 1883–1940* (London: Croom Helm, 1977), pp. 53–70. For a comparison of scouting and the Wandervögel, see John R. Gillis, *Youth and History: Tradition and Change in European Age Relations 1770–Present* (New York: Academic Press, 1974), pp. 149–55.

# Notes

33. See Rudolf Ekstein, "In Quest of the Professional Self," in *Twelve Therapists*, ed. Arthur Burton (San Francisco: Jossey-Bass, 1972).

34. Siegfried Bernfeld, "Die Psychoanalyse in der Jugendbewegung" (1919), originally published in *Imago* 5 (1919): 283–89; reprinted in Bernfeld's *Antiauthoritäre Erziehung und Psychoanalyse*, 3 vols., ed. L. von Werder and R. Wolff (Frankfurt: März Verlag, 1971), pp. 794–801.

35. See Gerhard Ziemer and Hans Wolf, *Wandervögel und freideutsche Jugend* (Bad Godesberg: Voggenreiter Verlag, 1961), pp. 439 ff.

36. Howard Becker, *German Youth: Bond or Free?* (London: Kegan Paul, Trench and Trubner, 1946), pp. 99–100.

37. Jones, *Freud*, 1:xiv.

38. For Bernfeld's activities see Philip Lee Utley, "Radical Youth: Generational Conflict in the *Anfang* Movement, 1912–January 1914," *History of Education Quarterly* (Summer, 1979), pp. 207–28. See also Gerhard Seewann, *Österreichische Jugendbewegung 1900 bis 1938* (Frankfurt: DIPA Verlag, 1971), 1:96.

39. Freud to Rudolf Olden (22 January 1931) cited in Rudolf Ekstein, "Siegfried Bernfeld 1892–1953," in *Psychoanalytic Pioneers*, ed. F. Alexander, S. Eisenstein, and M. Grotjahn (New York: Basic Books, 1966), p. 425. For additional biographical information see Hedwig Hoffer, "Siegfried Bernfeld 1892–1953," *International Journal of Psychoanalysis* 36 (1955): 66–71; Peter Paret, "Preface," in Bernfeld's *Sisyphus* (Berkeley: University of California Press, 1973), pp. ix–xxvii and Ilse Grubrich-Simitis, "Siegfried Bernfeld," *Psyche* 35 (1981): 397–434.

40. Max Hodann, *History of Modern Morals*, trans. S. Browne (New York: AMS Press, 1976). In the series that included Fenichel's essay, Hodann advanced typical left-wing youth-movement arguments: the youth movement must link up with working class youth and redevote itself to achieving "social community." See his "Vom Weg der Jugend," *Schriften zur Jugendbewegung* (April 1916), pp. 3–11.

41. O. Fenichel, "Sexuelle Aufklärung," *Schriften zur Jugendbewegung*, ed. M. Hodann (May 1916), pp. 52–60.

42. O. Fenichel, "Statischer Bericht über die therapeutische Tätigkeit 1920–1930," in *Zehn Jahr Berliner Psychoanalytisches Institut*, ed. by Deutschen Psychoanalytischen Gesellschaft. Forward by S. Freud (Vienna: Internationaler Psychoanalytischer Verlag, 1930), pp. 13–19.

43. In an autobiographical aside, Fenichel indicated that this schema did not fit his own youthful experiences, but he gave no details ("Sexuelle Aufklärung," p. 54).

44. "Sexuelle Aufklärung," p. 60.

# Notes

45. O. Fenichel, "Wedekind's Frühlings Erwachen," *Der Neue Anfang* 2, no. 3 (February 1920): 34–41. *Der Neue Anfange* succeeded *Der Anfang* ("The Beginning") which originated among a group that included Bernfeld, Wyneken, and Walter Benjamin. To deflect criticism that this new journal was his mouthpiece, Wyneken explained in the first issue that he did not control its editorial policy; see Gustav Wyneken, "Erklärung," *Der Neue Anfang* no. 1 (1 January 1919): 2. For a discussion of Wedekind and the youth movement, see Roy Pascal, *From Naturalism to Expressionism: German Literature and Society 1880–1918* (New York: Basic Books, 1973), pp. 222–28.

46. Frank Wedekind, *Spring's Awakening*, trans. Tom Osborn (London: John Calder, 1978), act 2, scene 2, p. 38.

47. O. Fenichel, "Sexualfragen in der Jugendbewegung," Siegfried Bernfeld Collection, YIVO Institute for Jewish Research, New York. The cover indicates that the manuscript was excerpted from the final chapter of a book with the same title. It probably dates from 1920, the year Fenichel delivered two lectures of this same title.

48. O. Fenichel, review of *Die Sexualethik der jüdischen Wiedergeburt. Ein Wort an unsere Jugend* by Hans Goslar, *Zeitschrift für Sexualwissenschaft* 6 (1920): 361–69.

49. Ibid., p. 365.

50. W. Laqueur, "The German Youth Movement and the 'Jewish Question,' " *Leo Baeck Institute Yearbook* 6 (1961): 193–205. See also Chanoch Rinott, "Major Trends in Jewish Youth Movements in Germany," *Leo Baeck Institute Yearbook* 19 (1974): 77–95.

51. See Philip L. Utley, "Siegfried Bernfeld's Jewish Order of Youth, 1914–1922," *Leo Baeck Institute Yearbook* 24 (1979): pp. 349–68.

52. Bernfeld to Martin Buber (14 September 1917), in Buber, *Briefwechsel aus sieben Jahrzehnten*, vol. 1: *1897–1918*, ed. G. Schaeder (Heidelberg: Lambert Schneider, 1972), p. 505. See also Chaim Schatzker, "Martin Buber's Influence on the Jewish Youth Movement in Germany," *Leo Baeck Institute Yearbook* 23 (1978): 152–53.

53. Willi Hoffer, "Siegfried Bernfeld and 'Jerubbaal,' " *Leo Baeck Institute Yearbook* 10 (1965): 159.

54. S. Bernfeld, "Eine Zeitschrift der juedischen Jugend," *Jerubbaal* 1 (1918–19): 2–3. Gershom Scholem, another contributer, resigned from the journal since he fundamentally disagreed with Bernfeld's plans for Jewish youth; see his "Abschied," *Jerubbaal* 1 (1918–19):125–30; the translation "Farewell," in Scholem's *On Jews and Judaism in Crisis* (New York: Schocken, 1978), pp. 54–60; and Scholem's *Walter Benjamin: The Story of a Friendship* (Philadelphia: Jewish Publication Society of America, 1981), p. 73, which outlines his relationship to Bernfeld.

# Notes

55. Fenichel is listed as a member of the *Korrespondenzblatt der Freunde des jüdischen Instituts für Jugendforschung-u. Erziehung*, no. 1 (August 1920). This newsletter described itself as including former participants of the Jerubbaal circle.

56. Fenichel, "Esoterik," *Jerubbaal I* (1918–1919): 467–73.

57. Branko Lazitch, *Biographical Dictionary of the Comintern*, "Kurella, Alfred" (Stanford, Calif: Hoover Institution Press, 1973), pp. 207–8.

58. Alfred Kurella, *Unterwegs zu Lenin. Erinnerungen* (Berlin: Neues Leben, 1967), pp. 16–29.

59. On Wyneken see generally Heinrich Kupfer, *Gustav Wyneken* (Stuttgart: Ernst Klett Verlag, 1970).

60. A. Kurella, "Für Wyneken," *Freideutsche Jugend*, 3 (1917):49. Kurella was not alone in moving from a Wyneken circle into the German Communist party; so did several other famous German Communists, such as Karl Korsch and Karl Wittfogel. See G. L. Ulmen, *The Science of Society: Towards an Understanding of the Life and Work of Karl August Wittfogel* (The Hague: Mouton, 1978), p. 17.

61. See Eugene Lunn, *Prophet of Community: The Romantic Socialism of Gustav Landauer* (Berkeley: University of California Press, 1973), pp. 249–53 and Lewis D. Wurgaft, *The Activists: Kurt Hiller and the Politics of Action on the German Left 1914–1933* (Philadelphia: American Philosophical Society, 1977), pp. 49–50. One of the contributors to *Der Aufbruch*, F. Bauermeister, together with Kurella, tried to keep Wyneken's followers unified by a series of round letters; see F. Bauermeister, H. Koch, and A. Kurella, eds., *Rundbriefe des Berliner Kreises*, no. 1 (December 1917).

62. F. Bauermeister, "Der öffentliche Betrieb," in *Absage und Beginn*, ed. F. Bauermeister, H. Koch-Dieffenbach, A. Kurella (Leipzig: Rodelli & Hille, 1918), p. 5.

63. A. Kurella, "Die proletarische Jugendbewegung," *Freideutsche Jugend*, 4, no. 11–12 (November–December 1918): 429–32.

64. A. Kurella, "Deutsche Volksgemeinschaft. Offener Brief an den Führerrat der freideutschen Jugend" (1918), reprinted in *Grundschriften der deutschen Jugendbewegung*, ed. W. Kindt (Cologne: Eugen Diederichs Verlag, 1963), pp. 163–79.

65. On Decisive Youth, see Eckart Peterich, "Über die Ursache des gegenwärtigen Zusammenbruches der deutschen Jugendbewegung," *Der Neue Anfang* 2, no. 7–8 (October 1980): 101–8.

66. A. Kurella, "Der Einzeln und die Gesellschaft," in *Absage und Beginn*, pp. 18–20. For a discussion of this pamphlet, see Richard Dorian, "Über den 'wesentlichen Lebensstil,'" *Der Neue Anfang* 2, no. 11–12 (December 1920): 164–65.

67. Knud Ahlborn, "Aus der Jenaer Tagung der entschiedenen Jugend-

# Notes

bewegung," *Freideutsche Jugend*, vol. 5, no. 12 (December, 1919), pp. 543–44. See also Karl O. Paetel, *Jugend in der Entschiedung. 1913–1933–1945*, 2nd ed. (Bad Godesberg: Voggenreiter Verlag, 1963), p. 51.

68. The most detailed account of Kurella's thought and actions is offered by a participant-historian, Fritz Jungmann [Franz Borkenau], and is included in the Frankfurt School volume *Studien über Autorität und Familie*, ed. Max Horkheimer (Paris: Librairie Félix Alcan, 1936), pp. 696–702.

69. Kurella presented his ideas in various periodicals; see his "Körperseele," *Freideutsche Jugend* 4 (1918): 235–52; "Körperseele," in *Die Erhebung*, ed. A. Wolfenstein (Berlin: Fischer, 1919), pp. 304–16; "Das Körpergefühl und sein Ausdruck," *Die Tat* 10 (1918–19): 508–11 and "Vom Körpergefühl," *Die Tat* 10 (1918–19): 715–17.

70. Fenichel, "Grundsätze zu jeder Sexualethik," in *Die Geschlechterfrage der Jugend*, ed. A. Kurella (Hamburg: Freideutscher Jugendverlag, 1918), pp. 30–37.

71. For a memoir of Luserke, see Hans-Windekilde Jännasch, *Spätlese. Begegnungen mit Zeitgenossen* (Göttingen: Vandenhoek and Ruprecht, 1973), pp. 95–104.

72. Martin Luserke, *Schulgemeinde. Der Aufbau der neuen Schule* (Berlin: Furche Verlag, 1919), p. 11.

73. Gustav Noske was the self-proclaimed "bloodhound" who led the violent suppression of revolution in Berlin; his name became synonymous with political repression.

74. Eckart Peterich, "Unsere Politik," *Der Neue Anfang* 1, no. 19 (October 1919): 306–8.

75. Fenichel, "Gedanken zu Luserkes Buch," *Der Neue Anfang* 1, no. 19 (October 1919): 309–11.

76. K. Marx, "Critique of Hegel's Philosophy of Right. Introduction," in *Early Writings*, ed. Q. Hoare (New York: Vintage, 1975), p. 251.

77. To compare the German: Fenichel, "Die Weltänderung sei radikal, sie greife an der Wurzel an. Die Wurzel ist der Mensch" ("Gedanken," pp. 310–11). Marx, "Radikal sein ist die Sache an die Wurzel fassen. Die Wurzel für den Menschen ist aber der Mensch selbst," "Zur Kritik der Hegelschen Rechtsphilosophie. Einleitung," in Marx/Engels, *Werke* (Berlin: Dietz Verlag, 1970), 1:385.

CHAPTER THREE / The Berlin Institute: The Politics of Psychoanalysis

1. Yela and Henry Lowenfeld as cited in Otto Friedrich, *Before the Deluge* (New York: Avon Books, 1973), p. 98.

# Notes

2. Wilhelm Reich, *People in Trouble* (Rangeley, Me.: Orgone Institute Press, 1953), p. 101.

3. Originally a clear distinction between Society and Institute did not exist; see Bertram D. Lewin and Helen Ross, *Psychoanalytic Education in the United States* (New York: Norton, 1960), pp. 4–6.

4. See generally Hans-Joachim Bannach, "Die wissenschaftliche Bedeutung des altern Berliner Psychoanalytischen Instituts," *Psyche*, 25 (1971): 242–53. Cf. Gerhard Maetze, "Psychoanalyse in Deutschland," in *Psychologie des 20. Jahrhunderts*, vol. 2, *Freud und die Folgen*, ed. D. Eicke (Zürich: Kindler Verlag, 1976), pp. 1145–79.

5. Wolfgang Huber, *Psychoanalyse in Österreich seit 1933* (Vienna: Geyer Edition, 1977), p. 6.

6. S. Freud, "Vorwort," in *Zehn Jahr Berliner Psychoanalytisches Institut*, ed. Deutschen Psychoanalytischen Gesellschaft (Vienna: Internationaler Psychoanalytischen Verlag, 1930), p. 5.

7. See generally John S. Peck, "Ernst Simmel 1882–1947," in *Psychoanalytic Pioneers*, ed. F. Alexander, S. Eisenstein, and M. Grotjahn (New York: Basic Books, 1966), pp. 373–83 and Ernst Lewy, "Ernst Simmel: 1882–1947," *International Journal of Psychoanalysis* 28 (1947): 121–23.

8. See Simmel's comments on "Sozialismus und Psychoanalyse" in *Der Sozialistische Artz*, 2 (1926); reprinted in *Marxismus. Psychoanalyse. Sexpol*, ed. Hans-Peter Gente (Frankfurt: Fischer, 1970), 1:24–29; his "Zur Geschichte und sozialen Bedeutung des Berliner Psychoanalytischen Instituts," in *Zehn Jahr*, pp. 7–12; "Die klinischen Möglichkeiten der Psychoanalyse" (Vortrag gehalten anlässlich der Eröffnung des Sanatoriums Schloss Tegel am 10. April 1927) (Manuscript); and his "Die psychoanalytische Behandlung in der Klinik," *Internationale Zeitschrift für Psychoanalyse* 14 (1928): 352–70.

9. E. Simmel, ed., *Anti-Semitism: A Social Disease* (New York: International Universities Press, 1946). This volume does not include all the papers from the conference.

10. Freud to Simmel (11 November 1928) in *Letters of Sigmund Freud*, ed. E. L. Freud (New York: McGraw-Hill, 1964), p. 383. See also Frances Deri and David Brunswick, "Freud's Letters to Ernst Simmel," *Journal of the American Psychoanalytic Association*, 12 (1964): 93–109.

11. E. Simmel, "Sigmund Freud: The Man and His Work," *Psychoanalytic Quarterly* 9 (1940): 174.

12. S. Freud, "Turnings in the Ways of Psychoanalytic Therapy," *Collected Papers* (London: Hogarth Press, 1957), 2:400–402.

13. János Paál, "Psychoanalyse in Ungarn," *Die Psychologie des 20. Jahrhunderts*, vol. 3, *Freud und die Folgen (II)*, ed. E. Eicke (Zurich: Kindler, 1977), p. 106; cf. Jean-Michel Palmier, "La psychoanalyse en Hongrie," in *Histoire de la psychoanalyse*, ed. Roland Jaccard (Paris: Hachette, 1982), p. 165.

# Notes

14. See Max Eitingon, "Berichte über die Berliner Psychoanalytische Poliklinik," *Internationale Zeitschrift für Psychoanalyse*, 8 (1922): 506–20 and E. Simmel, "Zur Geschichte und sozialen Bedeutung des Berliner Psychoanalytische Instituts," in *Zehn Jahr*, pp. 7–12.

15. M. Eitingon, *Zweiter Bericht über die Berliner Psychoanalytische Poliklinik* (June 1922 to March 1924) (Leipzig: Internationaler Psychoanalytischer Verlag, 1924), p. 4.

16. E. Jones, "Max Eitingon," *International Journal of Psychoanalysis* 24 (1943):191.

17. According to Richard F. Sterba's recent memoir, *Reminiscences of a Viennese Psychoanalyst* (Detroit: Wayne State University Press, 1982), Vienna also boasted an unofficial and slightly heretical Children's Seminar. He does not mention the Berlin Children's Seminar, but, given that the names are the same, and the contents similar, it seems unlikely that there was no relationship between them.

18. "Bericht über das Kinderseminar" (January 1927) (Manuscript).

19. E. Simmel, "Otto Fenichel," *International Journal of Psychoanalysis* 27 (1946): 70.

20. O. Fenichel, "Bericht über das Kinderseminar" (Manuscript). It is somewhat difficult to reconcile these two accounts, although it is possible both contain part of the truth. Fenichel's version comes from a brief lecture prepared for an official institute event. While its facts are doubtlessly accurate, it is possible that he omitted the real reason for Eitingon's suggestion. Simmel, recalling the inception of the seminar years later when diplomatic niceties were purposeless, may have factually inaccurate but essentially correct; even if the suggestion came from above, it was a response to the unhappiness of the younger left-wing analysts led by Fenichel.

21. A brief account by some disenchanted visitors to the Children's Seminar can be found in Lewin and Ross, *Psychoanalytic Education*, pp. 325–26; this account attacks as authoritarian one of its leaders, apparently Schultz-Hencke; he became a neo-Freudian; see Dieter Wyss, *Depth Psychology: A Critical History* (London: George Allen and Unwin, 1966), pp. 286–97. For a critique of Schultz-Hencke's concessions to nazism, see Helmut Thoma, "Die Neo-Psychoanalyse Schultz-Henckes," *Psyche* 17 (1963): 44–79, 81–128. Cf. Franz Baumeyer, "Zur Geschichte der Psychoanalyse in Deutschland," *Zeitschrift für psychosomatische Medizin und Psychoanalyse* 17 (1971): 203–40.

22. Edith Jacobson, "Annie Reich," *International Journal of Psychoanalysis* 52 (1971): 335.

23. Gustav Regler, *The Owl of Minerva* (New York: Farrar, Straus and Cudahy, 1959), p. 143.

24. S. Bernfeld, *Sisyphus or the Limits of Education* (1925); reprint (Berkeley: University of California Press, 1973), p. 64.

# Notes

25. O. Fenichel, review of "Sozialismus und Psychoanalyse" by S. Bernfeld, *Imago*, 14 (1928):386. "Sozialismus und Psychoanalyse" has been reprinted in *Marxismus. Psychoanalyse. Sexpol*, ed. H.-P. Gente (Frankfurt: Fischer, 1970), 1:11–29; a variant text appears in Bernfeld's *Antiauthoritäre Erziehung und Psychoanalyse*, ed. L. von Werder and R. Wolff (Frankfurt: März Verlag, 1971), pp. 490–97.

26. Apart from Fenichel himself, Edith Jacobson (1897–1978) is the best known of the circle, having established a reputation as a prolific and original theorist. Her influence and work in the United States has been described by Otto Kernberg as "profound," especially in the area of object relations. See Kernberg, "An Overview of Edith Jacobson's Contributions," and the volume in which it is included, *Object and Self: A Developmental Approach: Essays in Honor of Edith Jacobson*, ed. Saul Tuttman et al. (New York: International Universities Press, 1981). For some biographical information see Edward Kronold, "Edith Jacobson 1897–1978," *Psychoanalytic Quarterly* LXIX (1980):505–8. The facts in this obituary occasionally diverge from those Jacobson provided in David Milrod's "Interview with Edith Jacobson," 27 April 1971 in the A. A. Brill Library, New York Psychoanalytic Institute. She was born in a small town in Upper Silesia; her father was a doctor; she attended medical school and received her degree in the mid-1920s. She proceeded to Berlin, completing her training at the Berlin Institute in 1929, and she participated in the Children's Seminar and left-wing psychoanalytic groups with Fenichel.

27. Annie Reich (1902–71) (née Pink) was born in Vienna; she participated in the Austrian youth movement, where she probably met Fenichel; he introduced her to Wilhelm Reich, her first husband. She and Fenichel remained lifelong friends. She obtained her psychoanalytic training in Vienna and moved to Berlin with Wilhelm in 1931. In 1933 her marriage collapsed, and with the two children she settled in Prague, where Fenichel moved two years later. In 1939 she emigrated to New York. Two years after her death a collection of her papers was published, *Psychoanalytic Contributions* (New York: International Universities Press, 1973) with a forward by George Gero, another member of the Fenichel circle; he described her as "first and foremost a brilliant clinician" (p. vii). The main source of biographical information on Annie Reich is the obituary by Edith Jacobson in *International Journal of Psychoanalysis*, 52 (1971):334–36.

28. Kate Friedländer (1903–49) (née Frankl) is fairly well known in England, where she settled. According to Barbara Lantos, who wrote a memoir of her ("Kate Friedländer 1903–1949," *Psychoanalytic Pioneers*, pp. 508–18), the Hampstead Child Therapy Clinic, associated with Anna Freud and Doris Burlingham, was originally Friedländer's "magnificent dream." Born in Innsbrück, Austria, she obtained her medical degree in 1926 and obtained

# Notes

several additional degrees during the course of her life. She entered the Berlin Institute in 1926 (where she was known by her first married name, Kate Misch); she also became involved with the problem of juvenile delinquency, a commitment she retained her entire life. One of her final works was on psychoanalysis and juvenile delinquency [*The Psycho-Analytical Approach to Juvenile Deliquency* (London: Routledge and Kegan Paul, 1947]. Wilhelm Reich esteemed a paper she wrote in 1932 (with her husband) as supporting his own work; Reich's "Der Urgegensatze des vegetativen Lebens," *Zeitschrifte für politische Psychologie und Sexualökonomie* (hereafter referred to as *ZPPS*) 1 (1934): 136–37, commended an article by Walter and Käthe Mische, "Die vegatative Genese der neurotischen Angst und ihre medikamentöse Beseitigung" (1932). Reich later accused Friedländer (Mische) of plagiarism, surmising that she was politically afraid to mention his work; see Reich's review of K. Mische "Die biologischen Grundlagen der Freud'schen Angsttheorie," *ZPPS* 2 (1935): 71–73. Some additional information can be found in Willi Hoffer, "Kate Friedländer," *International Journal of Psychoanalysis*, 30 (1949): 59–60.

29. George Gero, born in Budapest in 1901, belonged to the periphery of the Lukás-Mannheim circles. His psychoanalytic training at the Berlin Institute, which commenced in 1924, was interrupted for a number of years while he obtained a doctorate in philosophy under Max Scheler. He returned to the institute in 1930; according to Reich, he participated in the smaller left-wing analytic discussion groups. He followed Reich to Copenhagen, where he remained until emigrating to the United States. My main source of information derives from a private interview with Gero, 9 September 1981, New York.

30. Little information is available on Barbara Lantos (?1894–1962). Born in Budapest (née Ripper), she participated in its radical student circles. She married a student named Lantos, a Communist who fled to the Soviet Union after the collapse of the Hungarian Soviet Republic. Barbara Lantos proceeded to Vienna and then to Leipzig where she was analyzed by Therese Benedek. In Berlin she participated in the Children's Seminar and Wilhelm Reich's group. She emigrated to Paris, then London. She wrote several articles on the instinctual bases of work. Biographical information has been culled from her own memoir of Kate Friedländer and from a letter to Russell Jacoby from Edith Ludowyk Gyömröi (9 March 1981).

31. Edith Ludowyk Gyömröi was born in 1896 in Budapest; a writer (under the name Edith Renyi), she moved in Mannheim's circles. She settled in Vienna, where she became very friendly with Bernfeld and his first wife. In the mid-1920s she moved to Germany (where she was known as Edith Glück). A member of the Communist party, she was expelled around 1934. She emigrated to Prague in 1933, and then Budapest, leaving in 1938 for Ceylon. Later she settled in England. My main source of information is

# Notes

Randi Markowitz's interview with Edith L. Gyömröi, August 1981, England.

32. The hostilities between Communists and Social Democrats set Reich against Bernfeld (and Federn). In 1932 Reich published "The Masochistic Character" (a revised version is in his *Character Analysis*, 3rd ed., New York: Farrar, Straus and Giroux, 1970). Reich criticized Freud's most recent formulation that masochism was a primary drive; for Reich the new theory was not only in conflict with the pleasure principle, it exchanged a sociological orientation for a pessimistic cultural philosophy; it posited a primary will of self-destruction. Freud sent a letter to the editors of the *Internationale Zeitschrift für Psychoanalyse*, who accepted Reich's essay. He stated that the Reich piece could not appear without a prefatory remark, declaring that its author belonged to the "Bolshevik party" which demanded total obedience to its dogma. (Freud's letter is cited in *Reich Speaks of Freud*, ed. M. Higgins and C. M. Raphael [New York: Farrar, Straus and Giroux, 1967], p. 155.) The implication that Reich's piece was party propaganda and the fact that essays by rank conservative analysts did not sport similar warnings caused a stir among some analysts. According to Reich (*People in Trouble*, pp. 147–48), Freud was dissuaded from insisting on the preface; in its place Bernfeld was summoned to refute Reich in an essay that appeared together with the Reich piece; see Bernfeld, "Die kommunistische Diskussion um die Psychoanalyse und Reichs 'Widerlegung der Todestriebhypothese'" *Internationale Zeitschrifte für Psychoanalyse* 18 (1932): 352–85; and the general survey in Helmut Dahmer, *Libido und Gesellschaft. Studien über Freud und die Freudsche Linke* (Frankfurt: Suhrkamp, 1973), pp. 332–35.

33. Interview with Edith L. Gyömröi, August 1981, England.

34. O. Fenichel, "Psychoanalysis and Metaphysics" (1923), *Collected Papers: First Series*, ed. H. Fenichel and D. Rapaport (New York: Norton, 1953), p. 26.

35. O. Fenichel, "Die offene Arbeitskolonie Bolschewo," *Imago* 17 (1931): 526–30.

36. André Gide, *Return from the U.S.S.R.* (New York: Knopf, 1937), p. 90.

37. Sidney and Beatrice Webb, *Soviet Communism: A New Civilization* (1935), 3rd ed. (London: Longmans, Green and Co., 1944), p. 484.

38. For two other enthusiastic accounts of Bolschevo, see Lenka von Koerber, *Soviet Russia Fights Crime* (London: George Routledge and Sons, 1934), pp. 98–120 and Ella Winta, *Red Virtue: Human Relationships in the New Russia* (New York: Harcourt, Brace and Co., 1933), pp. 206–10.

39. David Caute, *The Fellow-Travellers* (London: Weidenfeld and Nicolson, 1977), pp. 99–100.

40. O. Fenichel, "Psychoanalyse der Politik. Eine Kritik," *Psychoanalytische Bewegung*, 4 (1932): 256–59.

41. Fromm's "The Method and Function of an Analytic Social Psychology: Notes on Psychoanalysis and Historical Materialism," is reprinted in his *Crisis of Psychoanalysis* (Greenwich, Conn.: Fawcett, 1971), pp. 138–62.

42. O. Fenichel, review of "Über Methode und Aufgabe einer analytischen Sozialpsychologie" by Erich Fromm, *Psychoanalytische Bewegung* 5 (1933): 88 and 92.

43. O. Fenichel, review of *Der triebhafte Charakter* by W. Reich, *Internationale Zeitschrift für Psychoanalyse* 11 (1926): 387 (hereafter cited as *Int. Z. Psych*). The Reich text is included in his *The Impulsive Character and Other Writings*, trans. G. G. Koopman (New York: New American Library, 1974).

44. O. Fenichel, review of *Sexualerregung und Sexualbefriedigung* by W. Reich, *Int. Z. Psych.* 16 (1930): 522.

45. O. Fenichel, review of *Geschlechtsreife. Enthaltsamkeit. Ehemoral* by W. Reich, *Int. Z. Psych.*, 17 (1931): 405.

46. O. Fenichel, review of *Die Funktion des Orgasmus, Int. Z. Psych.* 16 (1930): 515–16 and 520–21.

47. O. Fenichel, review of "Dialektischer Materialismus und Psychoanalyse" by W. Reich, 17 *Imago* (1931): 132–37; reprinted in H.-P. Gente, ed. *Marxismus. Psychoanalyse. Sexpol*, pp. 31–36.

48. W. Reich, "Dialektischer Materialismus und Psychoanalyse," *Unter dem Banner des Marxismus*, 3 (1929): 736–71; reprinted in Bernfeld, et al., *Psychoanalyse und Marxismus*, ed. H.-J. Sandkühler (Frankfurt: Suhrkamp, 1970); English translation in Reich, *Sex-Pol: Essays 1929–1934*, ed. L. Baxandall (New York: Vintage, 1972), pp. 1–74.

49. For a survey see Joseph Wortis, *Soviet Psychiatry* (Baltimore: Williams and Wilkins, 1950), pp. 71–102.

50. O. Fenichel, *Hysterien und Zwangsneurosen* (1931) (Darmstadt: Wissenschaftliche Buchgesellschaft, 1967), p. 9.

CHAPTER FOUR / Exile: The Secret Freudians and Their *Rundbriefe*

1. Lucy S. Dawidowicz, *The War Against the Jews: 1933–1945* (New York: Bantam, 1976), p. 65.

2. Hannah Tillich, *From Time to Time* (New York: Stein and Day, 1974), pp. 153–55.

3. *Zeitschrift für politische Psychologie und Sexualökonomie* 1, no. 1 (1934), p. 87 (hereafter cited as *ZPPS*).

4. Among the best of the many biographies of Reich available are: David Boadella, *Wilhelm Reich: The Evolution of His Work* (New York: Dell, 1975); Constantin Sinelnikoff, *L'Oeuvre de Wilhelm Reich*, 2 vols. (Paris:

# Notes

Maspero, 1970); and Myron Sharaf, *Fury on Earth: A Biography of Wilhelm Reich* (New York: St. Martin's, 1982).

5. Wilhelm Reich, *The Invasion of Compulsory-Sex Morality* (New York: Farrar, Straus & Giroux, 1971); W. Reich, *Mass Psychology of Fascism* (1933), trans. Vincent R. Carfagno (New York: Farar, Straus & Giroux, 1970). The English editions of Reich's works often fundamentally diverged from the earlier German editions.

6. Arthur Koestler in *The God that Failed*, ed. Richard Crossman (New York: Bantam, 1959), p. 38.

7. *Reich Speaks of Freud*, ed. Mary Higgins and C. M. Raphael (New York: Farrar, Straus & Giroux, 1967), p. 44.

8. Richard F. Sterba, "Unpublizierte Diskussionsbemerkungen," *Jahrbuch der Psychoanalyse* 10 (1978): 214.

9. See chapter 3, note 32.

10. Tens of thousands of Jews migrated from Galicia, a Polish province of Austria-Hungary, to Vienna in the latter part of the nineteenth century. See Anson G. Rabinbach, "The Migration of Galician Jews to Vienna, 1857–1880," *Austrian History Yearbook* 11 (1975): 44–55 and M. Henisch, "Galician Jews in Vienna," *The Jews of Austria*, ed. Josef Fraenkel (London: Valletine, 1967), pp. 361–73.

11. Grete Bibring recalled being a medical student at the University of Vienna, when a fellow student, Otto Fenichel, announced a study group on sexuality and analysis; on her suggestion, two other students, Wilhelm Reich and Edward Bibring, joined, and they all went to visit Freud; see Sanford Gifford, "Grete Lehner Bibring: 1899–1977," *International Psychoanalytical Association. Newsletter* 10, no. 3 (September 1978), p. 9.

12. W. Reich, *People in Trouble* (Rangeley, Me.: Orgone Institute Press, 1953), pp. 102, 185–86, 197.

13. Ilse Ollendorff Reich, *Wilhelm Reich: A Personal Biography* (New York: Avon, 1970), p. 47.

14. Edith Ludowyk Gyömröi, "Recollections of Otto Fenichel" (Manuscript).

15. For instance, interviews with Sandor Rado, 1964–65, by Dr. Bluma Swerdloff, Oral History Research Office, Columbia University; interview with Edith Jacobson, 1971, by Dr. David Milrod, Abraham A. Brill Library, New York Psychoanalytic Institute.

16. See generally Randolf Alnaes, "The Development of Psychoanalysis in Norway," *The Scandinavian Psychoanalytic Review* 3 (1980): 55–101.

17. Reich to Rado, 1 May 1933, *Reich Speaks of Freud*, p. 168.

18. Cited by Reich in his response to Federn, 18 April 1933, *Reich Speaks of Freud*, pp. 163–65.

19. Reich to International Psychoanalytic Publishers, 17 March 1933, *Reich Speaks of Freud*, pp. 159–61.

# Notes

20. See the comments by Robert Fliess in his anthology *The Psychoanalytic Reader* (New York: International Universities Press, 1969), p. 104, which reprints several of Reich's papers.

21. David Boadella, *Wilhelm Reich*, p. 120

22. Reich to Opposition Analysts, 16 December 1934, *Reich Speaks of Freud*, p. 196.

23. Reich, *People in Trouble*, p. 180.

24. *Rundbriefe* (April, 1934) cited in *People in Trouble*, p. 185.

25. Reich to Opposition Analysts, 21 July 1934, *Reich Speaks of Freud*, p. 188.

26. Reich, *People in Trouble*, p. 185.

27. Reich to Opposition Analysts, 21 July 1934, *Reich Speaks of Freud*, pp. 185–86.

28. Reich to Opposition Analysts, 16 December 1934, *Reich Speaks of Freud*, pp. 196–98.

29. *Rundbriefe* (April, 1934) cited in *People in Trouble*, p. 188.

30. O. Fenichel, "Zu Reichs Buch 'Massenpsychologie des Faschismus'" (Manuscript). The manuscript contains a series of discussion points, probably for a seminar; for instance, "Why has the petite bourgeoisie previously been underestimated?" "How false or accurate is the formula that 'National Socialism is a petit-bourgeois phenomenon?'" "What is the 'bourgeoisification' *(Verbürgerlichung)* of the proletariat?"

31. W. Reich, "Experimental Investigations of the Electrical Function of Sexuality and Anxiety" (1933), *The Impulsive Character and Other Writings*, trans. G. G. Koopman (New York: New American Library, 1974), pp. 139–90.

32. O. Fenichel, *Problems of Psychoanalytic Technique*, trans. D. Brunswick (New York: Psychoanalytic Quarterly, 1941), pp. 105–6. See also the discussion of Reich in "Concerning the Theory of Psychoanalytic Technique," in *Collected Papers* 1:334–39.

33. See Samuel A. Guttman, "Robert Waelder 1900–1967," *International Journal of Psychoanalysis* 50 (1969): 269–73.

34. Robert Waelder, review of *Zeitschrift für Politische Psychologie und Sexualökonomie*, reprinted in *Marxismus. Psychoanalyse. Sexpol*, ed. H.-P. Gente (Frankfurt: Fischer, 1970), p. 188; originally in *Imago*, 20 (1934): 504–7.

35. O. Fenichel, "Über die Psychoanalyse als Keim einer zukünftigen dialektisch-materialistischen Psychologie," *ZPPS* 1 (1934): 43–62.

36. "Der Ausschluss Wilhelm Reichs aus der Internationalen Psychoanalytischen Vereinigung," *ZPPS* 2 (1935): 57–58. No author is given, but it is obviously Reich.

37. "The Drive to Amass Wealth" was finally published in *The Psychoanalytic Quarterly* and reprinted in Fenichel's *Collected Papers* 2: 89–108.

# Notes

38. As one of Freud's reactionary acts, Reich lists his "removal" of Fenichel as an editor of the *Internationale Zeitschrift für Psychoanalyse* "because he would not suppress the left" (*Reich Speaks of Freud*, p. 181).

39. "Bericht über die Fortschritte der Psychoanalyse in den Jahren 1909–1913," *Jahrbuch der Psychoanalyse* 6 (1914): 263–424. For an earlier survey, see Karl Abraham, "Bericht über die österreichische und deutsche Literatur bis zum Jahr 1909," *Jahrbuch für psychoanalytische und psychopathologische Forschungen* 1 (1909): 575–94.

40. *Bericht über die Fortschritte der Psychoanalyse in den Jahren 1914–1919*, foreword by Otto Rank (Leipzig: Internationaler Psychoanalytischer Verlag, 1921).

41. O. Fenichel, "Fortschritte der Psychoanalyse 1930 bis 1936." (Manuscript) pp. 1–2, 19, 28.

CHAPTER FIVE / Psychoanalysis and Its Discontents: Freudians Against Freudians

1. Ernest Jones, *The Life and Work of Sigmund Freud*, 3 vols. (New York: Basic Books, 1953), 3: 200ff (hereafter cited as Jones, *Freud*).

2. Freud to Binswanger (9 October 1936), *Letters of Sigmund Freud*, ed. E. L. Freud (New York: McGraw-Hill, 1964), p. 431.

3. See Jones, *Freud*, 3: 186. See the account of the meeting between Freud and Boehm in Richard F. Sterba, *Reminiscences of a Viennese Psychoanalyst*, p. 155 ff.

4. Edith L. Gyömröi, "Recollections of Fenichel" (Manuscript).

5. Jones, *Freud*, 3: 188.

6. Edith Jacobson, "Observations of the Psychological Effect of Imprisonment on Female Political Prisoners," in *Searchlight on Delinquency*, ed. K. R. Eissler (New York: International Universities Press, 1949), pp. 341–68.

7. See Marie Langer, "Psychoanalyse—in wessen Dienst?" *Neues Forum* 28, no. 213 (1971): 39–42 and her "Psicoanálisis y/o revolución social," *Cuestionamos*, ed. M. Langer (Buenos Aires: Granica, 1971), pp. 259–60.

8. Abram Kardiner, *The Individual and his Society* (New York: Columbia University Press, 1939).

9. E. Fromm, "Die gesellschaftliche Bedingtheit der psychoanalytischen Therapie," *Zeitschrift für Sozialforschung* 4 (1935): 365–97.

10. O. Fenichel, "Psychoanalytic Remarks on Fromm's Book *Escape from Freedom*," *Collected Papers* 2: 260–77.

11. E. Jones, "Evolution and Revolution" (1939), in his *Psycho-Myth, Psycho-History: Essays in Applied Psychoanalysis* (New York: Stonehill, 1974), pp. 254–75.

12. Leo Rangel, "A Neglected Classic: Otto Fenichel's 'Problems of

# Notes

Psychoanalytic Technique,' " *Journal of the Philadelphia Association for Psychoanalysis* 7, no. 1–2 (1980): 93–102.

13. O. Fenichel, "Über die Psychoanalyse als Keim einer zukünftigen dialektisch-materialistischen Psychologies," *Zeitschrifte für politische Psychologie und Sexualökonomie* 1 (1934): 43–62 (hereafter cited as *ZPPS*). English translation: "Psychoanalysis as the Nucleus of a Future Dialectical-Materialistic Psychology," *American Imago* 24 (1967): 290–311. The editor's introduction to this translation, which states that the essay has never previously been published and dates from the 1940s, is obviously inaccurate.

14. See Helmut Dahmer, *Libido und Gesellschaft* (Frankfurt: Suhrkamp, 1973), pp. 332–35.

15. W. Reich, *Charakteranalyse* (1933), p. 240; *Character Analysis*, 3rd ed. (New York: Farrar, Straus & Giroux), p. 214.

16. O. Fenichel, "A Critique of the Death Instinct," *Collected Papers* (New York: Norton, 1953)1: 370–71.

17. See generally Ernest Bornman, *The Psychoanalysis of Money* (New York: Urizen, 1976).

18. Sandor Ferenczi, "Zur Ontologie des Geldinteresses" (1914), in *Bausteine zur Psychoanalyse*, vol. 1 (Bern: Hans Huber, 1964) and "The Ontogenesis of the Interest in Money," reprinted in Bornman's *Psychoanalysis of Money*.

19. O. Fenichel, "The Drive to Amass Wealth," *Collected Papers*, 2: 103, 107.

20. "Elements of a Psychoanalytic Theory of Anti-Semitism," *Anti-Semitism*, ed. E. Simmel (New York: International Universities Press, 1946).

21. Ibid., p. 32.

22. "Psychoanalysis of Antisemitism," *American Imago* 1 (1940): 39.

23. O. Fenichel, "Psychoanalytische Einfälle zu Engels 'Deutscher Bauernkrieg' " (Manuscript).

24. E. Fromm, "Sozialpsychologischer Teil," *Studien über Autorität und Familie*, ed. M. Horkheimer (Paris: Librairie Félix Alcan, 1936). The other two introductory essays were written by Horkheimer and Herbert Marcuse.

25. O. Fenichel, "Fromm, Erich: Autorität und Familie. Librarie Félix Alcan, Paris, 1936" (Manuscript).

26. O. Fenichel, "Über Psychoanalyse, Krieg und Frieden," *Internationales Ärztliches Bulletin* 2 (1935): 39.

27. Edward Glover, *War, Sadism, and Pacificism* (London: George Allen and Unwin, 1933). Reply and counterreply in *Internationales Ärztliches Bulletin* 2 (1935): 76–77. The Fenichel essay and replies are reprinted in O. Fenichel, *Psychoanalyse und Gesellschaft*, ed. C. Rot (pseud.) (Frankfurt: Roter Druckstock, 1972), pp. 132–46.

# Notes

28. O. Fenichel, "Psychoanalyse und Gesellschaftswissenschaften" (1938), ed. R. Jacoby and R. Markowitz, *Psyche* 35 (1981): 1055–71.
29. O. Fenichel to Gisl Stein (24 October 1938).
30. René Fischer, "Zur Geschichte der psychoanalytischen Bewegung in der Tschechoslowakei," *Psyche* 29, no. 12 (1975), p. 1128.
31. "Psychoanalyticka Skupina v. C.S.R. (Psychoanalytische Arbeitsgemeinschaft in Prag) 1938" (Manuscript).
32. Fischer, "Psychoanalytischen Bewegung in der Tschechoslowakei," p. 1129.
33. The group included Paul S. Epstein, Professor of Theoretical Physics, and Richard C. Tolman, Professor of Physical Chemistry and Mathematical Physics, both from the California Institute of Technology.

CHAPTER SIX / The Illusion of a Future: Political Psychoanalysis in the United States

1. For a history of Topeka, see Douglass W. Orr, "Some Psychoanalytic Reminiscences," *Journal of the Council for the Advancement of Psychoanalytic Education* 1, no. 1/1 (1981?): 26–32. "Ernst Lewy . . . wore a kind of Homburg hat that Karl [Menninger] wanted him to discard because it looked 'foreign' " (p. 28).
2. Martin Grotjahn, "Recollecting Some Analysts I Knew: Otto Fenichel," *Bulletin of the Southern California Psychoanalytic Institute* 49 (June, 1977): 11.
3. Max Eastman, *Einstein, Trotsky, Hemingway, Freud and Other Great Companions* (New York: Collier Books, 1962), pp. 128–29.
4. *Psychoanalytic Theory of Neurosis* (New York: Norton, 1945), p. 586.
5. Ibid., p. 589.
6. Nathan Berman, "The Making of Soviet Citizens," *Psychiatry* 8 (1945): 35–48.
7. Katia Mann, *Unwritten Memoirs* (New York: Knopf, 1975), p. 123.
8. Leo Lowenthal to Russell Jacoby (24 June 1981).
9. "Remarks on Fromm's *Escape from Freedom,*" *Collected Papers* 2:264.
10. See Fenichel's abstract of Horkheimer's "The End of Reason" in *Psychoanalytic Quarterly* 12 (1943): 606.
11. See generally A. K. (Albert Kandelin) "The Psychoanalytic Study Group," *Los Angeles Psychoanalytic Society/Institute* 6, no. 4 (February, 1970): 3–7 and his "California's First Psychoanalytic Society," *Bulletin of the Menninger Clinic*, 30 (1966): 351–57.
12. E. Simmel, "Banquet Speech: 10 Years Celebration of the Psychoanalytic Group of Los Angeles, October 5, 1945" (Manuscript).
13. See generally Robert P. Knight, "The Present Status of Organized

# Notes

Psychoanalysis in the United States," *Journal of the American Psychoanalytic Association* 1 (1953): 197–221.

14. See J. L. Rubins, *Karen Horney* (New York: Dial Press, 1978); this split was followed by one led by Rado; see G. E. Daniels and L. C. Kolb, "The Columbia University Psychoanalytic Clinic," *Journal of Medical Education* 35 (1960): 164–71.

15. Fenichel submitted a statement on the question of multiple institutes to a 1942 Chicago meeting convoked by Menninger; see O. Fenichel, "Reflections on Training and Theory (1942)," ed. R. Jacoby and R. Markowitz, *International Review of Psychoanalysis* 9 (1982): 155–61.

16. See Sigmund Gabe, "Highlights in the Development of the Southern California Psychoanalytic Society and Institute," *Bulletin of the Southern California Psychoanalytic Institute* 43 (September, 1975): 7–11. Cf. Samuel Eisenstein, "The Birth of Our Institute," and Walter Briehl, "The History of the Los Angeles Society Split," both in *Bull. S. Cal. Psych. Inst.* 42 (April, 1975).

17. O. Fenichel to Leo Felix (2 October 1945).

18. Max Horkheimer, "Ernst Simmel and Freudian Philosophy," *International Journal of Psychoanalysis* 29 (1948): 112. Horkheimer noted that Adorno shared the ideas of his address.

## Chapter Seven / The Americanization of Psychoanalysis

1. Herbert Marcuse, *Eros and Civilization* (1955) (New York: Vintage Books, 1962), pp. 195–97.

2. Jerome Greenfield, *Wilhelm Reich vs. the U.S.A.* (New York: Norton, 1974), p. 250.

3. Martin Jay, *The Dialectical Imagination: A History of the Frankfurt School and the Institute of Social Research, 1923–1950* (Boston: Little, Brown and Co., 1973), p. 88.

4. Frank J. Sulloway, *Freud, Biologist of the Mind: Beyond the Psychoanalytic Legend* (New York: Basic Books, 1979), pp. 488–95.

5. Freud as cited in Theodor Reik, *From Thirty Years with Freud* (New York: Farrar and Rinehart, 1940), p. 138.

6. Joel Kovel, "Things and Words," *Psychoanalysis and Contemporary Thought* 1 (1978): 31–32.

7. Harold Bloom, "Freud's Concepts of Defense and the Poetic Will," in *The Literary Freud,* ed. Joseph H. Smith (New Haven: Yale University Press, 1980), p. 23.

8. Bruno Bettelheim, "Freud and the Soul," *New Yorker,* 1 March 1982, pp. 52, 53.

9. Nathan G. Hale, Jr., "From Berggasse XIX to Central Park West: The

# Notes

Americanization of Psychoanalysis, 1919–1940," *Journal of the History of Behavioral Science* 14 (1978): 310.

10. Robert P. Knight, "The Present Status of Organized Psychoanalysis in the United States," *Journal of the American Psychoanalytic Association* 1 (1953): 218–19.

11. Maxwell Gitelson, "Psychoanalyst, U.S.A., 1955," *American Journal of Psychiatry* 112 (1956): 700.

12. Maxwell Gitelson, "On the Identity Crisis in American Psychoanalysis" (1964), in his *Psychoanalysis: Science and Profession* (New York: International Universities Press, 1973), pp. 383–416.

13. Maurice Levine, *Congrès International de Psychiatrie, Paris, 1950: Trends in Psychoanalysis in America* (Paris: Hermann, 1950), p. 57.

14. Martin Grotjahn, "On the Americanization of Martin Grotjahn," in *The Home of the Learned Man: A Symposium on the Immigrant Scholar in America*, ed. J. Kosa (New Haven: College and University Press, 1968), p. 53.

15. Burton J. Bledstein, *The Culture of Professionalism* (New York: Norton, 1976), pp. 92–93.

16. S. Freud, *The Question of Lay Analysis*, trans. J. Strachey (New York: Norton, 1969), p. 97.

17. Clarence P. Oberndorf, *A History of Psychoanalysis in America* (New York: Harper & Row, 1964), p. 182. For an excellent discussion of the repression of psychoanalysis from an international perspective, see "Warum die Psychoanalytiker so ungern zu brennenden Zeitproblemen Stellung nehmen," by the Swiss psychoanalyst and ethnologist Paul Parin in his *Der Widerspruch im Subjekt* (Frankfurt: Synidkat, 1978).

18. S. Freud, *The Question of Lay Analysis*, p. 112.

19. Walter C. Langer to Sanford Gifford (17 February 1976) in their "An American Analyst in Vienna during the *Anschluss*, 1936–1938," *Journal of the History of Behavioral Science* 14 (1978): 53.

20. See Martin Shapiro, *Getting Doctored* (Kitchener, Canada: Between the Lines, 1978).

21. Joel Kovel, *The Age of Desire: Reflections of a Radical Psychoanalyst* (New York: Pantheon, 1981), p. 18.

22. See Nancy A. Roeske, "Women in Psychiatry: A Review," *American Journal of Psychiatry* 133 (1976): 365–72; Beverly C. Morgan, "Admissions of Women into Medical Schools in the United States," *The Woman Physician* 26 (1971): 305–9; Carol Nadelson and Malka Notman, "Success or Failure: Women as Medical School Applicants," *Journal of the American Medical Woman's Association* 29 (1974): 167–72; Rudolph Blitz, "Women in the Professions, 1870–1970," *Monthly Labor Review* 97, no. 5 (1974): 34–39; and Roscoe A. Dykman and John M. Stalnaker, "Survey of Women

Physicians Graduating from Medical Schools, 1925–1940," *Journal of Medical Education* 32 (1957): 3–38.

23. Laura Fermi, *Illustrious Immigrants: The Intellectual Migration from Europe 1930–41* (Chicago: University of Chicago Press, 1968), p. 170.

24. Ibid., p. 5.

25. The substance of this report, obtained under the Freedom of Information Act, has been blackened out.

26. Henry Pachter, "A Memoir," *Salmagundi* 10–11 (1969–1970): 36.

27. As recounted by Gertrud M. Kurth to Ernst Simmel (10 September 1946).

28. See W. R. D. Fairbairn, "The Sociological Significance of Communism Considered in the Light of Psychoanalysis," *British Journal of Medical Psychology* 15, pt. 3 (1935): 218–29.

29. Karen Horney, *New Ways in Psychoanalysis* (New York: Norton, 1939), p. 12.

30. Fenichel sent a letter to Paul Goodman commending his "The Political Meaning of Some Recent Revisions of Freud," *Politics* 2 (1945): 197ff. (Fenichel to Goodman, undated). Fenichel did not share Goodman's enthusiasm for Reich or anarcho-syndicalism; nor did he accept Goodman's designation of psychoanalytic revisionism as New Deal psychology. "My impression is that the political 'analogy' to Fromm is not represented by the New Deal, but rather by much more rightist movements in which it was usual to put on a 'left' appearance."

31. Norman Mailer, "The White Negro" (1957), in *Advertisements for Myself* (New York: G. P. Putnam, 1976), p. 300.

32. C. Wright Mills, *White Collar* (1951) (New York: Oxford University Press, 1973), pp. 148, 136.

33. C. P. Oberndorf, *History of Psychoanalysis in America*, p. 207.

34. For a brief discussion of Baran and Mills, see Peter Clecak, *Radical Paradoxes: Dilemmas of the American Left, 1945–1970* (New York: Harper & Row, 1973).

35. Robert M. Lindner, *The Fifty Minute Hour* (1955), introduction by Max Lerner (New York: Bantam Books, 1979). This edition is listed as the "33rd printing." The cover states "over 1½ million copies in print."

36. Lindner, *Rebel without a Cause* (New York: Grove Press, n.d.), p. 2.

37. Lindner, *Stone Walls and Men* (New York: Odyssey, 1946).

38. Lindner, *Prescription for Rebellion* (New York: Grove Press, 1962), pp. 30, 32.

39. Ibid., p. 42

40. Lindner, "Who Shall Practice Psychotherapy?" *American Journal of Psychotherapy* 4 (1950): 442.

41. Lindner, *Must You Conform?* (1956) (New York: Grove Press, 1971), p. 80.

# INDEX

# Index

# Index

# Index

# Index

# Index

# Index